Ca

Copyright © 2003 Jonathan Brown
All rights reserved.

ISBN 1-58898-945-3

To order additional copies, please contact us.
BookSurge, LLC
www.booksurge.com
1-866-308-6235
orders@booksurge.com

Caught With My Pants Down

Jonathan Brown

greatunpublished.com
Title No. 945
2003

Caught With My Pants Down

Table Of Contents

Byproduct of My Product	1
A Poem Should	6
To Mandy	7
Unrequited Love	9
Joke	10
What Were You Thinking?	11
Back Then	12
Third Highest Held Value	14
Press On But Digress	15
Twelve	16
B The Dishwasher	17
Two And A Half Year Old Revolution	18
After The Rain	19
I'd Bite My Tongue	20
The Lawnmower Is Coming	21
The American Dream	22
Chaos	23
Batten The Hatches	24
Lock Your Door	25
When The Bombs Drop	27
The Far Cry	30
? Everything	33
The Name Game	34
Lazy Zen Poem 1	35
I'm Sitting At My Desk	36
Lazy Zen Poem 2	37
Helium	38
Feet Speak	39
Love Your Computer	40
Dolphins Are Good Luck	42
Bad Acid Trip	44
Reflections Before My 21st	46

Reflections Of The Girl At The Festival	48
Promise me	50
Peaceful as	51
Passion for life	52
American Flag Condoms	53
You're An Angel	54
Early Mornings	55
Let Me Let Go	56
Written With A Secret Agent.	57
Funeral Procession	60
Cummings Is Hungry	61
Blinks Just His Left Eye	62
Great Expectations	63
Travel On	66
You Can't Tell Time	68
Slinky	71
1 2 1 2	74
Smile	76
Gradual Lean	77
Waffle House Intro	78
I'm Not Going To Lose My Arm	79
I Stare Off Into Nothing	80
Died In The Waffle House	82
One Waffle House Waitress	84
Lazy Zen Poem 3	85
Shy Smile Who Caught Me Staring	86
Jellybeans	87
Was It A Lie?	88
This Town Has Changed	89
Sincerity	90
I Was About To Get On A Plane And Come See You And Then You Said You Just Got Back With Your Ex-Boyfriend	91
1/03/02 Written With Specific People In mind	93
What's Your Favorite Color?	96
I Miss You Much	97
Indecisive Lover	99

Get Over It	101
This Is What 2—Minute Voicemails Do To The Opposite Sex	102
Me, Pussy, and Death	104
Shitting While It's Raining	105
The Time I Put My Foot Up A Radio Station's Ass	106
When I Take A Shit	110
Catcher In The Rye	113
Lazy Zen Poem 4	115
I Just Broke Up With Myself	116
Suppose	118
The Fight Inside	119
Rally In The Valley Of The Garden Of Good And Evil	120
Why Do Kids Start Drinking Early?	123
An Addict In London Told Me This	124
The Lord Is My Shepard	125
Lazy Zen Poem 5	127
Some Pussy And A Poem	128
Any Town In America	129
North Carolina Leaves	130
Yum Yum	131
Waiting On A Storm To Come	132
The Sun Rise Crew At A Beach House	134
Food Poisoning On The Way To New Orleans	136
Lazy Zen Poem 5	138
Nothing But A Condom And My Socks On	139
Lunch at Crunch Time	140
Motorcycle Accident	141
Lazy Zen Poem 6	142
A Gold Digger's Ecstasy	143
Just Another Puppet	145
Questions	147
To Private 3rd Class With Love	149
I Wish I Would Shut Up	151
Tribute To Poets	154
Words of Wisdom That Didn't Come Out Right	155

Ben	156
Car Wreck	158
On The Third Shelf	159
The Phone Doesn't Ring Much Anymore	160
Exams	162
Fake	163
Lazy Zen Poem 7	164
A Moment Of Silence	165
Follow The Person In Front Of You	167
A Revolution Televised	170
Give And Take	174
Honkey Pimps	175
Gluttony	176
Ignorant Virgin	177
After A Late Night In London	179
Lazy Zen Poem 9	180
Imagine A Nation	181
Dear Allison	184
Do You Believe In Monogamy?	186
Lazy Zen Poem 10	188
Cory	189
3 hookers	191
Lazy Zen Poem 11	193
Dark At A Young Age	194
I Drove Past Your House	197
You Got A Life To Live	200
We All Fall In Line	203
Alone	204
Lazy Zen Poem 12	205
The Problem With War	206
Lucky	207
That Night I Educated Myself	209
This Is Not A Good Poem	211
Beautiful Robot	213
Shit Happens	214
W	218
Waffle Prose	219

Gloria	221
Severe Eye Contact With An Old Soul	224
Dirty House	226
Lazy Zen Poem 13	227
Mardi Gras?	228
H.S.T. Concept in New Orleans	229
Lazy Zen Poem 14	230
Hot Sex	231
Questions Of Death	232
Solace Through Spoken Word	234
Body Language	237
Rise	238
My People Are Poets	240
In A World Of Pimps And Hoes	242
Is He Gay?	244
Ground Control To Lost Soul	246

This book is dedicated to all the people out there in the world.

Byproduct of My Product

She lost respect
For the opposite sex
At the age of five
When she went to the hospital
Bleeding from foster father's
Fingers inside

I knew her when she was eighteen
When she was a user, but not quite a fiend

One night
I was rolling a blunt
In the bathroom of a club
When I got done
I got up
I opened the door

Then she passed through
With eyes black and blue
Said she caught a beat down
From trick that was into crystal
He lost his shit and pulled a pistol
He robbed her
Raped her
And left her naked
That was yesterday

Today she's shaking
And aching for a fix
Asks me if she can hit my stash
And I said yeah baby
If you need some yee', page me

Here's my number
I'll call you back and help you out with that

Because under the umbrella
Of supply and demand I'm a man
Who's high on the food chain
I learned the rules of the game early
I slung weight at a young age
But never played with gunplay
Cause I was serving in suburbia
And working with jerks
That didn't have the capital

The thing about me,
I always had the start up fee
I was never hard up for anything
I always had enough to eat
I just want to run the halls
Of my college like thugs run the streets
I want to be the H.N.I.C.

MDMA is where the money is made
Ecstasy let's me be an independent
Entity within the business industry
And I am a businessman
Living in an
Elizabethan
Mansion
Stacking mad cash
From bagging grass
To cutting coke
To fucking hoes for payment

I'm a man with a plan
To survive in the private sector
I'm not hand to hand
I'm Fed Ex't by my connections

I don't hold a nine
Cause I don't see the heat
Campus police protect me from creeps
That seem to be drug dealers

Racial profiling is good for my business
Would you ever suspect me?

But something has got to be done
She doesn't think
She's gonna make it past twenty one
So young
And already succumb to hopelessness
I don't think she's ever getting over it

She's burning trees with eternity
And freebasing with Satan
Special K isn't for breakfast anymore
She's got holes in her brain
From rolls and cocaine

And I saw her the morning after she overdosed
Her stone eyes stared past me
Sober as a ghost
She was suicidal talking bout
How she's gonna find the bible
Pleading to Jesus
To please just
Ease this
Empty feeling

I saw her kiss the wall with her face
And taste withdrawal

There's no regulation on my methods
And no stopping my profits
She's hopped up on speed

And obviously
Dirty bags of pills fill the dance clubs
Which fill the girls with their hands up
Which fill the emergency rooms
Soon doctors will urgently pump the stomachs
Of thirteen college prospects
Just looking to have a good time

News flash
MDMA isn't regulated by the FDA
So if you buy drugs
At a night club
It might have stuff
That'll do more than fuck you up
People put bleach in speed
I put Windex on weed
Strict 9 in the spine
From the line just snorted
The effects of ecstasy have been reported
And it's important to be cautious
When dealing with a substance
That will make your brain look like
A piece of swiss cheese
Alzheimer's at eighteen

But she never did the research
All she knows is
This
Is what fixes what hurts?
She's hooked now and can't put it down
And that's a byproduct of my product

I do what I do
For status
For cabbage
For maximum cash
And to capitalize on habits

I give bags of lye
To frat guys
Who rag on crack heads
For their lack of prestige
And that's funny
That Kappa should've have seen
What was in his bag of weed
That's a byproduct of my product

Picture a white collar, high dollar pusher
See I'm not nitty gritty
Nor living in the inner city
But sitting pretty in the center
Of the suburbs, serving worse than herb
In your neck of the woods
To your children

And she could be your daughter
She could be your sister
Don't forget to be a father
Got a baby better kiss her

Cause a hug from a loved one
Goes a long way on a long day
She could be anybody
She could be you

A Poem Should

A poem should
drive and stop emotion,
love and hate the writer,
and take the reader deeper
than introspection or drugs ever could.

To Mandy

When I get the will to say I love you
The world will end

When you get over your ex-boyfriend
I'll move on to the next toy
And
Consider you only to be a friend

When I find what is behind
Your glowing eyes and get the will
To let you know that you
Are special

By that time,
I'll be gone
And by and by
By the time
I buy the time
To sell you truth
Youth will fade
And you will say
That it was a lie.

A crush from nothing–
Is far better than ever
Because it's a crush from nothing–
And something makes you blush

But alas
You're living in the past
And I'm living in your past
And my presence has no place in the present

But what if I live in the future?
What if by the time you
Figure out you're beautiful -
I'm gone –

Unrequited Love

she said there is
nothing more painful
than unrequited love.

I said, "yes there is"
smoothing your scrotum
out against a porcelain
bathtub and then Smashing
your balls with a rubber mallet
is more painful
than unrequited love.

shit, I'd rather lose some good pussy
than have my nuts beaten into applesauce.

I should have seen this coming
fuck, it was running up to me
like a three legged dog.

this cute little tripod
licked my knee
and bit my balls
and held on like an
alligator to a sheep.

I should have seen this coming.

Joke

PART of the PROBlem with DRINKing is PISSing,
you START to TIP back a COUPle of COLD
ONES and THEN you SPEND HALF
of the TIME HOLDing it BACK. It seems LIKE

I'm COOL, but REAlly I NEED to
TURN AROUND and PISS in the TUB
with MY SECond DICK. MY
BLADDER MIGHT BURST

RIGHT this inSTANT. inciDENts LIKE this have
HAPPened while CRAPping. I ONCE
took a SHIT a MONTH BEhind Schedule.
I JUST TOOK a PISS

With my THIRD DICK. WHEN i was a KID
I could HOLD a PISS forevER I didn't
have to USE a BRUISED FINGer to
HOLD it. and WHERE did I get ALL

THESE DICKS? i THINK it CAME
from a JOKE i HEARD aBOUT HOW
MANy DICKS a MAN could THROW
at a BITCH. HIS WORDS WERE,

"I would THROW a WHOLE BAG
of DICKS at a BITCH," HE SAID.
and the REAson MY FINGers HURT
is beCAUSE I BIGHT them. i CAN'T

STOP

What Were You Thinking?

the drill drilled.
and all you heard was the drill.

the dentist's mask smelled
like a cloth
gauze.

it's a weird feeling
when your eye balls
turn around
and look at your brain
to see what you were thinking.

Back Then

Back then we were all crazy poets in a madhouse
We hung our madness on coat
Racks like sweaty hats that
We'd worn all day

Back then we put our fingers in blenders
And bull frogs in our armpits
Back then we attracted flies with dog shit
And we drank hog piss until the wee
Hours of the moonset

Back then we licked telephone poles
In the cold and we got stuck just so
We'd have some stability
We did it just to stop running.

Back then we drank banks
And got our checks cashed in dive bars.

We followed our vice until
Somewhere inside of us
A prostitute was arrested

And we rested for nobody
Not even ourselves.

We lived in a hell we created
We visited Babylon on a daily basis.

Our friends in the daylight
Sent us postcards from heaven.

And we followed the recipes
That were passed down to us
And we loved to fuck
And we drank too much
And we escaped our crowded nightclubs
To cardboard boxes where we wouldn't
Have to pick fights.

And in the middle of it all
We lived life on the edge.

Third Highest Held Value

I'm alive in a time
where society tries to commit suicide.
Vivid lies contrived by
political infidelity.
Tell me if it's just me
but apathy has to be the third
highest held value
behind fear and laziness.
Give me a beer,

Press On But Digress

It's frightening to do the right thing
When bullets spit over bullshit

Followers lose faith

When hit men are heroes
And
War criminals are senators

The stepped on and depressed
Will press on but digress

Lifeless sellouts
Spell out life sentences

And

Budget cuts cut the throats of those in need.

Twelve

I was
Twelve years old
With a cold beer
In a turtle shell
Gripping a pack of smokes
Outcasted
I didn't care
I was out
Getting blasted

I was in
The eighth grade
Blazing eighths
With a head
Full of acid
After classes
I'd stay dazed
Until way late
In the evening

And now
At twenty
I wake up
After drinking
All night
And I think
If I sip another
Drink
I just may
Shit my liver.

B The Dishwasher

B
The dishwasher

?
if
the

Dish listens
when the wat

Er gets here.

and the cup
boards open

Meow

my eyes are big

Two And A Half Year Old Revolution

I asked my two and a half year old nephew
what he wants to be
when he grows up
He said I want to be a shotgun Uncle Jon
Buck Buck
the revolution starts with us

He raised a fist with his left wrist
and waved a middle finger with his right

He took a swig from his sip cup
and passed the apple juice

He said it's time we attack the Establishment

He said he was sick of baby food
He wanted more chocolate
and later bedtimes

and then he pooped his pants and smiled

He told me that we were going to take down
the man but it's hard to do that
With stank in his pants

So I changed his stanky draws.

After The Rain

I defended sin as long as I could see heaven in the distance. I missed the mark and kicked my heart to the curb to further my pursuit in the Garden of Eden. I was tempted by Eve but I decided to find my own tree. So in my solitude I called you. And you picked up the receiver when I dropped a line only to find that I was divided by the times of the present and the past. And as soon as I heard your voice I declined to ask for the future. I wasn't distraught that you bought a new identity cause I fought, fought for the cause. And I sold what I lost. And I found what I put down years ago. And there were tears poured for freedom and believing in living. Now I'm seeing the reason that
I'm seeing the reason.
I'm seeing the reason that I left in the first place,
the day I flipped the page and started a new chapter.
After the rain
    The sun must shine

After the night
    The day breaks darkness

The starving must eat
    And the sleepy must rest.

I'd Bite My Tongue

I'd bite my tongue
but I swallowed it
when I ate my words
a while ago

I need to sleep but I keep
my eyes open so
I can see the night

I don't mean to turn my back
but I only have eyes
in the front of my head
and I want to see everything
that's happening behind me

The Lawnmower Is Coming

Fuck it,
Let's burn the clouds
Down
And give the sky something
To cry about

The growing grass lives in fear
Of the lawnmower

The lawnmower
Is
Coming

The American Dream

if I can't
scare you
into being
an American

if I can't
bribe you
into being
an American

well wait

maybe I can
scare you
into being
an American

Chaos

I walk down Meeting Street

and parking meters
talk to me.

They ask me
if I got
some change.

Their faces
say
out of order.

and I wonder
where all this
chaos comes from.

Batten The Hatches

Forget your roots.
Be a freestanding tree
that needs no dirt.
An everlasting burning bush
turns eyeballs to look backwards
and presses wax between
the grooves of the medulla oblongata.

Who would of thought once habitable
mindscapes escape brainwaves
and become destitute and less acute?
The stream of consciousness
trickles in the middle
of a clear cut forest
once laden with the Trees
of Knowledge.

It's a call to arms
from a man with no sea legs to stand on.
Batten the hatches.

It's a mantra chanted in a different language.
It's a plate of meat in front of a vegan.
It's the long jump in a wheel chair.
It's doing the twist with a sprained ankle.
It's a neutered cocker spaniel humping
a chihuahua in missionary position.

Lock Your Door

Lock your door.
Wrap duck tape
around your mouth.
Silence what you know is right.
Eat what they feed you.
Believe deceiving secrets.
Broadcast to the masses.
Condemn the protestors
pastors and jackasses.
Blast Korean made firecrackers
on the Fourth of July.
Pour some lies
in a wine glass.
It's time we sit down
and concede to be passivists.
What happens nxt
is out of our hands.
Clutch a cell phone
hit redial
and tell home
you might be out for a while.
Set the dial on the network news.
Sing the blues.
Drink a few drinks if you please
but please ease up
on the freethinking.
We don't need it.
This is a team effort.
We are protecting your civil liberties.
Free speech needs
an apple in its mouth
a honey glaze

and a hot poker in its ass.
Kneel down under your desk
it will stop the radiation.

When The Bombs Drop

I apologize to all the guys
Who have fallen and died
But the sky will fall
Before bombs bring peace
More like pieces of first born son
To mom's front doorstep.

American pride is a lie
I was there when it died
And I ask you
Where you going when the bombs drop?
And the worst hell is a fifteen year old kid
In the armed guard
Where you going when the bombs drop?
And the church bell is the alarm clock
Wake the fuck up.

This is not a just war
This is just a prestigious war
This is not a war on terrorism
It's imperialism, serial killing.

But through the kindness of our hearts
We stayed hardnosed through trade embargoes
And starved those millions of children
That while I'm talking
We're still killing
In the name of billions of dollars
Our four fathers had this concept in mind
When they justified slavery
Fuck you, pay me
Human life isn't worth the bottom line

And Saddam Hussein had the same idea
So who's sane?
We're both of the same vein
Mainline the pipeline
To sustain and maintain
A status of having more than you can pay for
Wage war for the price
Of convenience store gas pumps
So I ask you
Is this a modern day jack move?
Is the red white and blue
Robbing to get paid
Pistol whipping competition
Leaving it black and blue?
The answer to that question is yes.

This is not a just war
It's just a prestigious war
This is not a war on terrorism
It's imperialism, serial killing.

The republican man grandstanding
On land stolen from Native Americans
Can't stand not to finish his daddy's war
It's a vendetta to defend an honor
That was never there.
And me and you are in the middle
Because the people will be used
As a sword and a shield
Hospitals will be liable for unidentifiable
Sores to heal
And who's to blame?
Don't these politicians know the
Rules of the game?
It's not cool to claim
That you're the biggest kid in school
Knowing good and damn well
The nerd can spell better than you.

These words serve a purpose
And that is
To ask the U.S. military service
To pull out
Wipe its dick clean
And stop fucking the rest of the world.

The Far Cry

Camel lights handle my oral fixation.
I ask the cashier
for a draft beer,
just a little social lubrication.

Barkeep,
bring me a Newcastle please.
I apologize JB,
all we serve is Pabst here.

I've been at this bar since last year
breathing tar fumes
and cheep perfume
from barflies
and raspy queers.

Pour me a drink barkeep
and keep um coming.
I sleep in the dump
Slumming
I summon drugs
from cut throat
Thugs.
I've seen a slut get her throat cut
Fucked and forgotten.
I've woke up from cold sweats, coughing.
I've woke up in a coffin
I opened the top
and walked out of my own funeral.

Now I wander the streets
a zombie covered in vomit.

I glare at the world through
the bottom of a stout glass.
I worry that my decrepit skeleton
might melt in the wind.
I got welts on my back from bronze buckles
attached to black leather belts straps.
I stumble backwards hunched over
and approach the ever encroaching future.

I am two loose front teeth
of a crack baby.

I have a necktie noosed
firmly around the nape of my neck.

I have a life sentence of nine to five
I am the guy that hates his job
I am the father that doesn't bother with his child.

I am a fifteen year old scared run away
hungry in a bus station.

I am the bound feet of a Chinese girl.

I am the twelve year old in a sweatshop
that sewed your Disney sweatshirt.

I am thirteen and knocked up by a nineteen
year old that gave me cold beer.
He told me he loved me
He told me he loved me
and now that my tummy is swollen
He acts like I'm ugly.

I am condemned by men that divide
Heaven and hell with scripture.
Make your exodus.

Exit this.
My existence is far from marginal.
I am the Liberty Bell
that when rang
fell on deaf cold shoulders
like acid rain.
I am the same as you
I am the same as you
I am the dark side of life,
the far cry.

I am strangely angry
Yet at rest when oppressed.

Even the sun shuns me.
Run from me.
I am the mirror that fears your reaction.
I am the time you got your ass kicked.
I am laughing at you

look in your past
and you will see that
you are exactly the same as me.

? Everything

cheddar and brie
elbows and bowties
milk and butter
macaroni and cheese
salt and pepper
OJ and eggs
coffee and sausage
bacon and biscuits
tasty but is it?

The Name Game

Do you ever have one of those moments
when you make a really
good connection with a girl
and it's not the first time?

Like this is a reappearing girl
whom you've seen more than once
except, the only problem is
you can't remember her name.

You're not even sure
she ever told you her name.

She calls you by your name.

But still, you don't know hers.

So you do the old
thing
where you introduce her
to one of your friends
with hopes that she will say
her name to him
but she doesn't.

Lazy Zen Poem 1

I'm walking up the stairs with cat food
Go find a metaphor

I'm Sitting At My Desk

I'm sitting at my desk on Sunday night
after traveling all weekend to slams.

On the way back to Charleston
my cat, Bananas, peed in the back seat.

My house has school paraphernalia
scattered about. Tomorrow I plan

to throw my irrelevant material
possessions away. But then again,

they are all irrelevant. I don't need
any of the shit I have. Then the big

question is, what do I need if
nothing I can touch means

much? I don't know.
I'm just going to keep reading

and writing and talking to positive
people who keep me on track.

Lazy Zen Poem 2

I bite my nails
And I scratch my head with pads
I listen

Helium

I breathe in deep on a helium balloon.
My voice gets higher.
I go back for another drag of the gas.
Soon I rise above the street level
among the pigeons and streetlights.

The full moon pulls the tides.
My eyes push the ground farther away.
The buildings down below look smaller.
Up here I can see palm tree canopies
From a different angle. They look
Like cool luke warm swarms of spiders.
Legs dangling,
spinning circular webs that ebb
and flow with the wind.
Palm trees blow with the wind.

I am plankton in the air rushing
with every gust of wind.

I've let go
but I haven't given up.

Feet Speak

My heart
beat throbs
in my feet

I've walked
city streets
for miles and
miles and

I still
get tired.

My feet
are tires
and the burnt

rubber blubbers.
My feet speak

in toe
tongues.

Love Your Computer

Who wants to study
when there is
somebody to fuck?

Who wants to fuck
when computers don't
get pregnant?

Soon we'll stick
our dicks in disk drives
and push strollers
filled with microchips.

i never wanted to disappoint you

i never
wanted to
disappoint you

i know
i didn't
meet your
expectations

but i always
made a point to
be ambitious

which is
what attracted you
to me
in the first place

Dolphins Are Good Luck

Lee Barbour told the artists in Charleston
to listen hard to the music in our heads

Because the best muse is the bird
within the ribcage. The heart
is where the art is.

I want to flood my rough drafts
with sand storms and
raise the stream of consciousness.

Intentions matter.
Happy thoughts manifest into physical existence.
What we say contains space.
Passion evaporates into the atmosphere.

There is so much out there
we cannot see.

I wish I had the ears of a dog
so I could hear a higher range
of frequencies. I frequently
think thoughts are not
as personal as fingerprints.

How many times have you looked
into your lover's eyes and you knew
what they were thinking?

Sometimes I think
thoughts
are not unlike a beehive.

We buzz by and land on whatever flower
tastes sweet, a flower we can trust.

I've always thought dolphins were good luck
and lighting bugs fire butts are kin to miracles
and housecats know all there is to know about Zen.

So then I want to be
a caterpillar when I write
and a butterfly when I let my poems fly
and a lion when I hold a mic
and as humble as
a humming bird when I spit a verse.

When it's all said and done
I'll walk down the steps,
open the door
and stroll in the rain
until I make my way home.

Bad Acid Trip

ok there it was.
bottom of the ninth.
two men on.
bases loaded.

and the pitcher
has a bad acid flashback.
he pictures himself underwater
with no oxygen tank.
he chokes.
he throws the ball
at the thick shadows
that creep up behind him.
the shadows have long pointy teeth.
their breath smells of french onion soup.

baseball has nothing
to do with anything anymore.

the mound begins to turn white
on top
as the pitcher stands on the mound
he can feel it squish down.
the mound seems irritated
and sensitive.
the pitcher leaps
as high as acid will take
him
he comes crashing down and smashes
puss out of the mound.

it's gooey

and soupy
and chewy
and chunky

covered in an oily film
of tapioca pudding the pitcher
regains composure
only to find that he has urinated on himself
but it's not urine, it's
amniotic fluid and
he just gave birth to a turtle
and inside of the newborn turtle shell
are cubes of cherry jello.

Reflections Before My 21st

I run around
cleaning my house.
I've had a week to do it
but I'm leaving town
in the morning.
Auditions in Atlanta,
camp on Monday
until Friday
I turn twenty one
on Thursday.

and I want to give a big thank you
to all the bartenders and waitresses
in Charleston who have
been serving me alcohol
while I was underage.
Thank you.
It completed my experience
and brought my smoky
nights full circle.

Without alcohol I couldn't be drunk.

I'm going to camp on Monday for a week.
Being a counselor is something
I look forward to every year.
It's almost like rehab for the spirit
and the bad habits,

It's
good vibes
mountain air

hard work
new people
hot food
rain, rain and
we still press through.

Camp Bob is a diving board
I jump off of every year.
I don't hit the pool until a year later.
The water is cool.

Reflections Of The Girl At The Festival

I went to this outdoor festival
called Eden Fest.
Everyone sleeps in tents
when they finally go to bed.
Pissing in porta-potties becomes
the normal thing to do.

It rained on Friday night,
the Wailers played,
I bobbed my head to
familiar reggae songs
and watched the hippie chicks
dance in the mud, barefoot.

I met a sweet girl, Misty
age 17
but she seemed mature
and she was funny and assertive.
Her gaze was curious but stern.
We walked and talked after the concert.

My teammate on the Greenville Slam Team
called my cell phone and told me
we were going to smoke a blunt with the Wailers
and I figured that was a good enough
reason to leave her company.
But when I met my teammate
I realized I should have stayed
and it turned out
the Wailer's tour bus's brake lights
could be seen in the distance and
we didn't get high.

Later that night I found
that sweet girl Misty again
and we drank blush with her
in her tent
while her slut friend made
out with my teammate.

The next day Misty read my palm
before I performed.
I had two shows on Saturday
and she saw both of them.
After the second show we hung out for a second
and then we parted ways.

I saw her again at a drum circle/bonfire.
She said her friend was making it with some dude
and she was tired and didn't know where to sleep.
So she just came down here
to see what was going on.
About 4 a.m. I walked her back to the teen tent
where she was going to sleep under the stars.
Before she passed out she gave me
her notebook and let me open it.

And to me, that act was much more intimate
and satisfying than if she opened her legs.
I was struck by her honesty and flattered
by how human the whole situations was.

I flipped through her journal
while she fell asleep
and then I walked back to my tent
in the darkness.

Promise me

When it's dark outside
look within.
When the walls close in
and it gets hard to breathe,
climb out of the top
and promise me you won't
live in fear. If following
your dreams means leaving
the practical reality
behind, let it mean that.
You are the only one
living in your skin.

Peaceful as

The world
will only
be as peaceful
as I am
because I
see the world
through my
eyes.

Passion for life

I got a passion for life
my appetite is
never satisfied.

I need a higher high,
a bigger plate,
another beer,
a smoke.

Another Book to read
and one more poem to write.
A blowjob
and some fucking.
A shower
and more fucking after that.

An all nighter.

American Flag Condoms

I wish they made
American flag condoms

So every time
I fuck somebody

I could thrust lust
like the U.S. draws blood.

You're An Angel

I hope you live a long life.
I hope you achieve all the things
you strive for. I hope
your life is filled with thrills and
excitement. I wish you
could fly as high as
your wings will take you.

Early Mornings

This zone is inhabitable
I need a stable
place to lay and wait.

I've been living two
lives by myself.
I need to take a break.

Too many late nights
ran into the break of day.
I've watched the sunrise
feeling the world spin underneath me
too many times.

Let Me Let Go

Let me let go
when I'm downright
uptight.

When I'm spent
defenseless but still
intense
in need of rest
depressed and torn.
I wish you would
rescue me
and mend my forlorn
poor and destitute
empty core.

Fill me up with
enough love
to make me whole again.
I told all my other friends to fuck off.
I'm stoned, stressed and so depressed
I need you
I look in the mirror and I don't believe what I see
I need you
I need you right now.

Written With A Secret Agent.

Wild jazz
mild claps
and muffled voices
sift through
shakers and
candle lit faces,
smiles exhale
replies.
And I sit
with a Guinness
and a secret agent
with a head full
of YES.

Shadows drifted
swiftly pressing
this pen through
the page
and into a
place
where breaks
in concentration
mean taking my eyes
off this candle lit
legal pad.

I weave
basket cases
into stuffed animals
shaped the way
dolphins make
ripples in the

film on top
of uncovered pudding
film. Reels spin
projecting large
smoke screen
images on ashtray
faces. Mirrors are
now glass and I
see myself outside
the lines of the highway
driving on the median
I sit halfway sideways
with my head out
of the car window.
Wind blows wet
around my baseball
cap hatted head.

I wear sunglasses
when I press my
face against the
microwave and watch
marshmallows melt
towards tall mushroom
clouds.

And the clouds wobble
as a hood ornament would
on a dashboard.
Here I can see myself
on the other side
of a picked scab.
The four cylinders
aren't running well.

The onions hunted
carrots below

and the carrots bellow
where the pineapples tell
how palm tree leaves
look at sundown
over the marsh.
Purple watercolors
stop off at the dock
for more oil
to cook with gas.

Pages turn in a closed book
and the spine plays
five card stud
at a black jack table
with Don King
and Mike Tyson.

Funeral Procession

Bison pull
Her son
In a hearse
Riding
To a funeral
Procession

Cummings Is Hungry

you know sometimes,
I come home after a hard day
and my cat is asking for food
and he says, "hello."
Cummings strolls in
in spats towards me. He

laughs and licks his paw

and he tells me that elephants
and white hills line Dover.

We both acknowledge
that he is a cat, and
yes, he just talked.
We both walk towards the cabinet
where the food is
and he pulls a toothpick
through a tuft in his fur
and he picks behind the canines
on the right side of
his mouth.

Blinks Just His Left Eye

Cummings looks up
blinks his eyes, meows,
and then blinks just his left eye.

His ears fold back
and he opens his mouth
and shouts, "We have fleas!
Look man, the weather is warming up
and, I don't know if you've noticed!
But my entire fur covered feline skin
is itchy! I used to be soft.
And now I'm irritated and I need lotion."

Great Expectations

Lead by example
Increase the volume
And eventually all of you
Will evolve into
An everlasting burning bush

If people passing turn and look
Don't question yourself
You have the answers
The second you second guess
And doubt yourself
You count yourself out
Believe in dreams, be strong
And be loud
Keep your self esteem
Even when the ground beneath
Your feet seems so hot it steams
Keep cool, even when people
You've just met disrespect
Or mistreat you, keep cool
Trust, love and respect
Are the three tools used
To fuel and fulfill
Great expectations
And that's what I have for you

Great expectations

The kids in front of me
Got big shoes to fill

Right now more than ever

The world needs you
So go
Be you

Everybody under the stars
Is an artist
And art is where the heart is
An artist must target the farthest
Part of the darkness
An artist must embark
On a journey
To the center of the skin
Where the heart is

And carve intentions on the heavens
Make a mark in the dirt
Build sandcastles that tower toward
The clouds and dance
In the rain as if you were a loose
Newspaper in the wind

Live life like you might die tonight
Pray before you go to sleep
The Lord made you
And the Lord will take you
Away in a heartbeat
So while you're here

Exhale bright lightning strikes
See through the eye of the storm
Be an everlasting burning bush
Thunderclaps after performances
You were born to make noise

And the kids in front of me
Got big shoes to fill
Who will find the cure for AIDS

Is it you?
Who will save the human race?
More importantly
Who will preserve the earth?
Is it you?
What about the hydrogen car?
You can do it.

I'm hoping Elijah's the next Beethoven

The kids in front of me
Got big shoes to fill

You will be the poets
You will be the thinkers
You will make the difference.

Travel On

My soul speaks
through the soles of my feet.
So if you have to, babble on
in Babylon but I can't dabble long.
I've got to travel on. I've got
a mouthful of poems
and a mapful of cities
and a backpack full of product.
I need to leave this town
get up, get out, and get something.

I daydream of the eighth Charka
where the spirit lies
and a man never dies
and the truth begins
and the rainbow ends.

Where awake and asleep
both float above being separated.
It's a place where people's thoughts matter.
Ideas occupy space and contain time
And the simple things we think
manifest into physical existence.

There was a mirror there.
I reached out
and touched the center of it.
Bouncing ripples waved off
not unlike sound waves.
This was a dream screen.
On the other side was a
smile in my mother's eyes

and my childhood from a past life
and all the while
time passes by.

You Can't Tell Time

I write love letters
To my ancestors
On parchment paper
With dove feathered quills
But still
I am oblivious to the obvious
Every minute minute is significant
But you can't really tell time
Anything.
Time is not listening
Time speaks a different language
Time answers to the sun and the tides
And the shadows that surround sun dials
So race against the clock man!
You got not a second to waste
In this secular wasteland
Smile and find God in the eyes of a wino
Smile blindfolded and know
That you see what you believe
That is why I am iambic
And manifest anapestic
Because I can't rest
Until I reach my left hand
Into my chest
Dig my heart out
And throw it at you.

Everything I know to be true
Up to this point is pointless
Because this is a lucid dream
And I am thinking happy thoughts.

My first words were bird chirps,
I was a starving kindergartner
In the Garden of Eden
Eating apple jacks
And drinking mango Snapple
While kicking back and relaxing
And snacking on a slice
Of the American Dream
Apple Pie.

In my dream Einstein's mind rhymed
That imagination is more important
Than knowledge, and that
Is a piece of knowledge in and of itself
And
Shines bright like halogen lights
Following me in my rearview.

My foot rose from the petal
And I slow down
To observe road signs from God
And she asked me why I started to write.
It started from my heart
This art started as a catharsis
I used it, even abused it
To get over hardships
I used it to shine light bright right
On darkness. I put the felt pen
To the page when I felt afraid
And faded back through the black
To find the light, the kind of light
That I missed in my blissful childhood.

That's why most of my early poems
Are filled with words of hurt
And dreams deferred
And mirrors feared
And tears unheard.

I started thinking about my future
And realized
Tomorrow is rocking a tarnished Figaro
And yesterday blazed cess for days.
That's why I'm amazed by the way
We state how we feel.

How is it real if what you feel
Is concealed by the ideal
Of what you wish was real?
If you need to heal
And it's not given with speed
Try to feel, find the real
The mind is proof
What you think- is truth
If you're loosing
The kind of focus
You need to find
Use the hoping or open mind
Be open to dreams that seem serene
And in the distance for instance.

Your wildest childish imagination
You want to be

BE.

And I will not die a victim
My death is not in vain
My pen is the sword
And the ink are bloodstains
I have slain the beast
The beast from within
And I will not die a victim
My death is not in vain
My pen is the sword
And the ink are bloodstains.

Slinky

The slinky is strolling slowly

  the slinky told me
    to slow down
      and hold out

The slinky stopped
 jingled
  and then hopped
on top
 of the top
  of the stairs
where
 he just slunk
down
  down
    below
the ground
  this slinky slunk
rung
 by
  rung
   down
    each rung
of the ladder
d
o
w
n
the train of thought
  this slinky hopped on
the tracks of a
    jazz thought process.

and we were in a harmonic
 demonic
  acoustic
   electronic
    mind
me and this slinky's thoughts
 were
  hooked
   on phonics

we flowed up and down
not left to right
not side to side
but both sets of knees buckled
   and I was in synch
with this slinky
and this slinky grew
some arms and feet,
   a head and legs
  soon out of aluminum- a
midsection grew
and this slinky was a nasty
jazz
musician

he exemplified the epitome
of a swift experienced talented
improviser

this slinky played the
bass, this slinky swung
drum sticks and stuck to
the licks he knew
as well as
spewed jazz
from the
d

e
p
t
h
of hell

to the
h
e
i
g
h
t
of the flight
of the dove
that flies above heaven
this slinky blew trumpets that called
for the sound of war

me, the slinky, and all of mankind
rhymed on mics.

The whole world was at the poetry reading
And the entire galaxy
Clapped

happily we
JAZZED.

1 2 1 2

heads bop
threads pop
pots hit with spoons
feet stomp
keep calm
preach on
reach beyond
pump your fist
raise a peace sign
heartbeats beat in unison
who would come to the gates
with anything but honesty
promise me
in the dark of midnight
your heart
starts to divide

on one side
is everything you ever knew
on the other side
is everything you need to learn

burn
hurt
jerk
shake
pray
lay down
say it now
stand up
hands up
leave yourself

thieve hell from the people
who personify it
take it and make
your exodus
raise a fist
blaze the rich
feed the pour with it

Smile

smile like the taste of a lime
with a straight spine
and the shine of
a polished dime
and the virtue
of an honest crime
and the sleep schedule
of a lion

Gradual Lean

when the band breaks
for a set
I will hand them a check
addressed
to the best

Waffle House Intro

yellow painted lines in the parking
lot

in the Waffle House

I cough and smell vomit
I'm ok

the cook coughs
and he talks with a low pitched voice
the phone rings

in the Waffle House

I'm Not Going To Lose My Arm

headlights pass my sight
on the right side

tables divide sides
bacon grease creeps up
refilling ketchup
and grinding coffee

knuckles on the cheek
I'm bored

my cigarette ash is long
and my water is not
filled up

I wrote a phone number on my arm

and said, "I'm not
going to lose my arm."

I Stare Off Into Nothing

I stare off into nothing
in front of me

I tap my foot
and close my eyes
and sit

"Do you want some
water?" "Thanks"

the night is masking fantastic rhythms
I'm managing damaging advantages

scandalous schemes
manic dreams
angels who sing
entangled web of a spider's web
and brown long hair
down there

amounts that don't stop
pounding astounding mountains
jiggling earthquakes

the earth takes a breather
the ground frowns and
opens up and we all jump in
humping someone close to us

Soapsuds

frozen snot on mountaintops

no beanie and I forgot my
jacket

Cell phone activated
Credit card authorized
Optimized Internet speed
Web site access

I left my cigarettes in the car.

me, the shakes, and God
because somewhere along the way
we have to believe that God is with us

Died In The Waffle House

It's crazy. People sit down
in the southeast
with Stetson hats
and black ostrich
boots
people out
and then in
and mingle
and sing jingles
in their own head
when they try to talk
to other people
headaches on a diagonal
level
low frequencies
besides the small beaded chain
hanging from the ceiling
two lights on
light bulbs encased
in a floating cream circles
hanging from the ceiling
yellow menus and fixed gazing
lists of shit to do
lists
created late recess

resuscitate, no breathing
EMS
sleep in a Best Western
when you can afford it
but this guy just passed out
blacked out

not responding
a note is tacked to the wall
as a reminder
PLEASE DON'T DIE
wait a second, I drank
four cups of coffee

where the sage is blazed
and the song is played
and people nod their head
to the beat of a flat line ------------

One Waffle House Waitress

she's only seventeen but she's
on her own
away from home
away from mom
she works third shift
blurred vision from
a blank customer
others talk shit
she spits insults
after a dude
referred to her
as a prostitute

Lazy Zen Poem 3

I need a beverage alchemist
To turn my coffee into beer

Shy Smile Who Caught Me Staring

as sweet as satisfaction
Ass is fat, and she
carries it like a backpack
If I could tap that,
I'd grin from chin
to temples.
This isn't meant to be an insult
it's just an impulse.
Pardon me,
but on a scale of one to ten;
You're a fifteen.
All others pale in comparison
I gave you an extra five
for fine thighs
and kind eyes
-It's embarrassing to get caught
Staring

Jellybeans

her skin was silk to touch
her tangled hair smelled
as sweet as mangos
her earlobes were
cold and tender
peach
jellybeans
that I nibbled

Was It A Lie?

I wrote my hotel room
on my hand-

-and diamond spoons-

I have hair
on my hands
from verisimilitude
truth

This Town Has Changed

this town has changed
I've been gone for two weeks
and it doesn't seem like
and it doesn't act like-
it's changed,
but in actuality, in all sincerity-
it has changed

more plastic, more crispy
less friendly, more bass in the cars
more strippers in the bars
less street corner musicians
the bums got meaner

the owner is sitting outside
of my favorite bar
but I'm underage

my friends invited me to another bar
but I'm underage

the crazy thing is
I'm overage or at least
I feel like I
am

Sincerity

Although sincerity is temporary
it is also eternal
that moment
those eyes
that second
those lips
it's all real
it's all now
and it's all forever
thieved memories will live longer
than red woods and like
a good red wine
memories get better with age
this is why sincerity is the most convincing
characteristic
because if it is genuine,
it is the most persuasive of all
human attributes

I Was About To Get On A Plane And Come See You And Then You Said You Just Got Back With Your Ex-Boyfriend

I'll admit
when you said you were back with Steve
I was a little-
I was a little and I was a lot
I was very and not much all in the same
I was jaded at first
and a little less elated to come see you
than I once was
because I thought it would be weird.
not that we weren't friends before anything else
and not
that we are not friends now,
only the whole thing
would have been a clashing of souls
Fuck This

I'm worried about you
cause I've been there
and if it's
off and on
and off is pain
and on is joy
and the extremes keep getting greater
then the joy you experienced,
that better than it ever has been feeling
will spoil as a gallon of milk spoils
and the pain will be filled with curds
stinky and putrid as a gallon of spoiled
milk is.

but it's your life not mine
you seem happy and you will probably
continue to be so.
I'm just tired of being a shoulder to lean on
I'm going to pull the banana soon
but you are not a possession to own
and I, I, I,
I will say I love you next time I mean it
and not hold back
but this world will keep spinning
spinning in rotisserie fashion!

1/03/02 Written With Specific People In mind

A played games with B
she got mad
he was sad
X had sex with Y
Y cries and screams why
did X sex H next?

die for love
cry for love

be wrong much of the time for love
lust sucks out the nuts
W busts
"troubled you much," says U
as she screwed another dude.

a few boo hoo
who knew a few got screwed
out of a tissue when Y was crying?

blinded by the light
sight is hindered by a
cold December's night
September's bold lies cut through
and sold thighs May's way
payday can't wait
what's the wage?
Fate
what's great?
sunshine and other things
but sometimes what is great, is fake

and artificial on the surface
pick up the serpents
live for a purpose
find what you lost
and if you can't find that
find a cause

find a cause for life
blinded, brained, maimed, minded
P's and Q's
see it through
please do
fall from a brawl
or be lifted up through it all
up into the heavens
rising like leavened bread

severed heads go rolling through the street
everyone I meet is rolling.
Blindfolded and scolded
by what the right hand was holding.
throw it in the Thymes River
if you got something to give her
deliver what you need
to give her in a letter.

for better or for worse
never let conversations be rehearsed
you can't reverse
the face in the situation
you're facing
if a mistake was made
and the correction is left for death
in a foreign land
handed by a folklore like hand
imaginary sad and scary demons
are breathing on the back of my neck

I lack respect for myself
if I'm not taking the next step.

What's Your Favorite Color?

What's your favorite color?

The color of your eyes.

What color are your eyes?
Green.
I mean I think it's green
It could be some others.

Clusters of big green mustard colored stars
Bright lights in the sky
It's pretty far off
But you can almost see Mars.

A quiet, silent, far off feeling
Comes beaming
Comes gleaming
Down like straight from the ceiling.

This is like fate was waiting
As far off in the distance as Mars.

A persistent fate that I'm feeling,
And it's so great to see her face
So close to my face in a place
Where I can taste the ways
Of how much time
We have left in this place.

Your breath next to mine
No time to waste

Smile sweetie, Everything's gonna be all right.

I Miss You Much

I miss you much
I miss your kiss and your touch
I wish I could see you
I wish I could please you
Great hips and tasty lips
Thighs that are pleasing to the eye
Let's go reminisce about Eskimo kisses
On a long night we hold each other tight
Nothing between us but skin and dreams of us
Run my fingers through your hair
Love lingers in the air

I know I've treated you bad and made you sad
But that doesn't change the love that we had
Or the feelings that I still have
It was perfect
We even went to church to worship together
Forever still,
I want to be the shelter in your bad weather
No one can ever fill your space
I can still see your face, and taste your kiss
I miss you much
I get pissed enough to go to fist a cuffs
With myself because of my pride
Pride can never override honest love
Promised from above.
I can never deny my heart
Or it's gone from the start
Right can never be wrong
Fights can never last long
And ties that are strong can never be gone
It's hard to go on

Because I'm still holding on
To the one that I'm sold on
I'm trying to say that I'm not a cold one
I remember the red dress
You wore to my after prom
I was so impressed
My jaw dropped and hit my chest
I was truly blessed to be
With best girl in whole world
Your hair was curly and surely
We were the happiest couple there
And before your prom, we ate at the Palms
It was a doubles affair.
I had no troubles and no cares
Because I was there with you.

Indecisive Lover

There seems to be some confusion
with the fusion of cupid and me and she.

I'm going to shed some light
on my hectic flight.
Breath deep, take heed, and take a seat
as I say these things.

Run away from me
and to me
when I say lose me
I mean take me.

Wait for me means
don't hesitate please.
Break up with me means
let's make up please.

I've lost my mind.
You can't buy love
it doesn't cost a dime
or find love
when you tried to lie
and call it lust
cause trust went bust.
I'm cussing and fussing over us
damn man I'm fucking up.

I locked locks on more
doors than I could afford
but then tried to pop those locks
on the locked doors

but what for?
I wanted more of you.

So why did I ignore you?
It hurt to bad
to think someone had
the first I had.

Get Over It

I will remember you wherever I go.
When I wake up I can smell you if I try to
But I said goodbye to you
And now I'm to shy to...
I'm to shy to cry, dude
Until I can't say, Oh Well.
People can tell when my emotions go to hell
The good old, sell me L Johnny comes back
And laughs at that
Get over it
It's not over yet
Life goes on
But strife lives long
And I carry this
With me
Shifty, Lift me
Come on are you with me
Do you want to share with me everything?
Do you want to carry me when I can't stand?
But, I don't like things handed to me.
Who plans to choose me
Who doesn't want to lose me?
GO!... No, I don't know.   Stay!...
I pray that you'll stay
I'll make way for a new day.
That's when you'd say, OK
I can't wait.
I can't even state how much this means.
This means she's going weep with me
And keep me safe
Look at me face to face
And pretend the past was never erased.

This Is What 2 — Minute Voicemails Do To The Opposite Sex

Obviously
hot and steamy
sweaty sloppy scromping
is fun enough.
But I fucked up
when I got down.

I busted my nuts
and I regret it now.

2 ½ minute voice mails
tell a tale
of tail that should have been
withheld.

I'm sorry I slipped up
and stuck my dick where it didn't belong.
My dong didn't know the difference
between commitment and slipperiness.
And now,
From the neck up I got a headache
from someone else's telephone call.
I wish I could put my cell phone
to my balls and let them talk.
Because my head is ready to cut off
all sexual relations.
I slipped up and slipped in
and now I need to defend my right
to be anonymous.
I promise those intimate minutes
meant everything in the moment.
But I need my freedom.

I'm a tomcat
that got scratched
by some good pussy.

Me, Pussy, and Death

Pussy was a pencil sharpener
Heart was a jellyfish
Tongue was a catheter
She smelled like she kissed

Grip was a venus flytrap
I, the fly trapped
   took a breath
and winked at the face
   of death.

The three of us
were gonna take a ride.

Shitting While It's Raining

It has been raining steady
all morning long
and I have to poop again.

So I sit on the throne
and I'm not sorry for
what I'm about to do. I
will poop

Oh Lord, I will poop.

The Time I Put My Foot Up A Radio Station's Ass

The reason I wrote this poem was because a local radio station advertised their open mic as a slam for months. I talked to some of the head people about how I thought it was false advertising. They agreed with me that it was false advertising, but they still were not going to change the advertisement broadcast. And yes, this poem is arrogant, and yes, I am waving my poetic dick around. I still think what I did was the right thing. Someone had to wake them up.

I write from the fire inside
that burns bright and ignites
high temperatured flames
that tempers iron into blades
made to slay
gas stations that betray the truth.

I'm putting my foot up your ass
because I asked if you wouldn't front
on your advertisement
but you declined my request.

I asked nicely once
and you continue to front.
Now you get confronted.

In good faith
how can you devalue
the very art from
you claim to have a heart for?

That's blatantly disgraceful
and nevertheless negligent.

You know better than to lie to your listeners.
My mission here is to state clearly-
if you love poet tree,
dig the root of it,
the precise lines and exact syntax.
Words are the coin of this realm,
you're bout to get taxed for counterfeiting currency.

A slam is 3 rounds, 3 minutes.
Intense bouts where proud poets
Get up and shout out loud.
Judges hold grudges,
five scorecards but only the three middle count,
time limit, bracket system,
egos get shattered
and one poet goes home
victorious.

The only thing that competes on this mic
each week
is which bitch's legs are as thick as peanut butter
and just as easy to spread.

The only thing timed on this mic
are the same lame
white jokes told by the host between poets.
Yo, your flow is about as fresh
as the discharge from a coat hanger abortion.

If George O' Fish was spitting this
he'd say you swallowed your mind.
All o' yall must have been giving Clear Channel
brain for so long, you forgot the difference
between right and wrong.

That's why I'm
playing renegade

and pulling the pin on the poem grenade
and throwing explosive flows
that blow the walls off this façade.

I'm bum rushing
sucker punching
you punks.
Jacking you
smacking you ass backwards
and snatching my word back.

You don't deserve to spit it.
You didn't earn this shit.
It turned personal when you purposely
used slam's name in vain.
I'm knocking the tower of babble down
you can get down on your knees
and suck my diction, corporate pawn.

Drink a latte while I slave away
picking the coffee beans.
9.43 is a drag cabaret.
slam is John Holmes or Ron Jeremy.

Even after I've gone home
I'm not going to be satisfied
until you take the fucking lie
off your advertisement.
Until that happens
I'm going to battle rap you bastards
every time I get on a mic
and I speak five times a week
in cities across the Southeast.

You don't believe me,
poets will protest in the streets.

Why do you lie
when you never studied PSI or NPS
nor do you know
what those acronyms mean.

How can you devalue the same art form
you claim to have a heart for?

You fucking fakers can sue me for slander.
I'm liable for libel cause this
utterance is getting published.

While the audience applauds
I'm going to grip my balls
and flick you off
for ripping off
the life I love.

Go pout bitch,
I just shit in your mouth.

As a result of this poem the advertisement was pulled from the airwaves. As a result of this poem I am also banned from the microphone at Level Two. Even after many apologies and months of absence they still won't let me hold the mic. I may have shot myself in the foot but it was a cause I believed in. And to the audience at Level Two, I miss yall. Don't worry, you'll see me again. The only regret I have is that I don't have a live recording of The Time I Put My Foot Up A Radio Stations Ass.

When I Take A Shit

When I take a shit
I look at the toilet
recoil
and break that bitch.

I take a deep breath
stare at my feet
and let logs ooze out.
Next I wiggle
bounce for the jiggle
and squeeze
plop
plop
brace my elbows at the knees
take another deep breath
flex
reach for the sky to get my spin aligned
and have a freestyle rhyme
session with my sphincter.

If it's a slight stinker
I'll light a match to diffuse the bomb.

Even on constipation I remain calm
rock back and forth and rotate
the crank to activate the play dough
machine.

I think we are having inch circumference
spaghetti.

I hold my ground firm in case of a
machine gun attack.

When my butt's mean
and doesn't want to be clean
and the runs come
I make sure to wait a few minutes
after the final blast at ground zero
because I don't want any straggler
seeping slowly out of the rectum

A defective session in the bathroom
is no laughing matter.
It can turn into disaster.
The key piece of the operation
is clean up duty after the dookie.

When I pootie
sometimes it's soft
and sometimes it's hard
but most of time its chewy.

Floaties require a second flush.
Prairie dogging, a quick rush
cause the rodent is poking out
of it's hole and corroding
the air quality only
adding skid marks
to once laundry fresh undies.

When I wipe
I use my right hand
and apply it to the top of the valley
and precisely and carefully after
the wheels touch the ground
I push heavy on the breaks so as not
to run off the runway onto the chodel

or grundel and god forbid
my muddy balls.

And I never retrace my steps.
It's not kosher to double dip.

Trouble with shit
or maybe the beauty of it
is, we all do it.
So the next time you conversate
with the opposite sex
and you have nothing to say
just discuss your poo
because it's something we all do.

Catcher In The Rye

If I could reconcile
all the disgruntled sex and smiles
and humble those
who fumbled with crumbling limmerence
and lies,
I would.

If I could lend a shoulder
when you folded when the other's shoulder
got colder than boulders
of ice,
I would.

If I could calm the rising
fire that rises red hotter
and higher than the bloodshot
eyes of a stalker,
I would.

I'd defend each and every
sincere fear that ears hear
and hearts feel and tears near
would dry up
and the innocent party
would find what made them
innocent in the first place.

The worst day of hurt
would be the first day of feeling.
The thirsty would be drinking,
The hungry would be eating.

The ignored and disregarded
would be needed.
And the pieces of the broken hearted
would be gathered and placed back together
and never be shattered again.

But the facts remain the same.
I'm going to keep going against the grain
and riding the waves of life
until they crash
and I'm buried underneath the sand.

Lazy Zen Poem 4

Nobody is a saint
until you die.

I Just Broke Up With Myself

Today I felt detached
like I broke up with myself
and it wasn't one of those
I never want to see you again,
you know you are doing the right thing
type of breakups.

Today it was like me and myself
just wanted different things out of life.

When I realized that I
let me go,
me wanted to stay.
Me was crying
and saying that he would change.

I told me
it's not you,
it's I.

All I could do was sigh
and hope that me would understand.

I might call me later
but I don't want me to get the wrong idea
like I want to get back together.

I just hope me is doing fine
and through all the arguing
I just wanted me to know
that we really did go good together.

When I see me walking down the street
I'm afraid it will be weird or awkward
because I'll want to run up and hug me
and give myself a kiss on the cheek.
But I know I shouldn't do that
because I just broke up with me

If you see me
tell him
I said high.

Suppose

If I could observe
the words of the universe
on an oversized overhead projector,
I would underline
all the come on lines of light.

Being alive would mean seeing
sun rays without eyes
and smelling the ocean
without a nose
and doubting nothing.

Suppose humans were in tune with
the moon as the waves
move with the tides.

The Fight Inside

Tired is no reason to stop.
Pain is no excuse.
Drive is the only factor involved.
Gain is what is produced.

A straight line is the quickest route
between two points.
So first an endpoint must be chosen
and next-
The best path.

Unnecessary baggage should be left
behind.
Keep your eyes on the finish line.

And keep in mind
the fight for life.
And keep in sight
the fight inside.

Cause the biggest battles
I ever fought
were in my own head.

Persistence mixes with
the catalyst of intentions
to form my existence.

Rally In The Valley Of The Garden Of Good And Evil

Rally in the valley
of the garden of good and evil.

I was there when almost
two hundred thousand
people supported the Iraq
war protest in DC.

Hope for the future?

Drop acid not bombs.

No taxation without representation.

Face it.
Face it.
Democracy is gone.
Republicans can suck
my stinky anarchist weenie.

Revolution was televised
after the fact on C Span.

See hams walking down the street
Holding hands with turkeys.
They walk into a milk bar
And order the hard stuff,
Chocolate.
Hocking up green lugies with
ravioli sized pimples
on their faces

dimples,
disgraces.
As punk rock music blares
in the background and cold stares
flare in the direction of the foreign people,
church steeples have poster boards
glued to them,
on the poster board is written
Nuclear War Is Good For The Poor.

We must move quiet.
We must be anonymous.
We must keep the promise
never to give up
or breathe much
because we move quiet through the night.

The boys in blue nor
the red white and blue
can stop the black and red.
This is the movement of revolution.

A revolver sits in the belt next to
tear gas packs behind the shield
under the helmet.
The police border the masses in riot gear.

Rally in the valley
of the garden of good and evil.

But what will it change?

All around the country
People, not schools, corporations or newspapers
but people! have been voluntarily silenced
to please their constituents.
If you have no balls I won't give you mine.

I suggest you use your youthful
Holy Shit I just blew spooge
on a computer screen mind and stand up.

I don't really take anything seriously.

Why Do Kids Start Drinking Early?

A twelve year old
looks at his dad's
glass of jack
and asks himself
why he holds it
with so much
confidence.

An Addict In London Told Me This

The good Lord
blessed us
with cess
and dust.
Thus don't
question.
Rust.

The Angel
of Death
will strangle
what's
left.

The Lord Is My Shepard

The Lord is my Shepard.

If the Lord is my shepard
temptation is a wolf.

When I close my eyes,
eyes see rose colored
flashes of light
bright firecrackers
ignite sparks that start blazes.

Life changing vibrations,
high level voltage pulses.
My pulse rate raises.
I raise my arms.

I cut my legs off
and hold my ankles above my head
and swing them like numb chucks.
I cum blood and shit food
and eat my words.
I will pull my ears off
and put them in your pocket
so you can hear what I hear here.

What are diamonds to a blind man?
He can't see.
I traveled light years camping in a tent
called skin.

I fall in a ditch and find diamonds.

I am invisible to a child behind bars
because Riker's Island holds
fourteen year olds in prison.
It's called home.

Family is food on the table.
You think money grows on trees?
Boy, I'm doing what I can
What's for dinner?
You were never there.
Go to your room.
I hate you.
I can't wait to.

Leaves fall before winter
and spring sent her
to mingle with the birds and the bees.

Picture me screaming for help cause
I had no dreams
but all I did was sleep.

I looked down at my bowl of cereal.
My eyes fell out of my head.
I through them behind the stove.
I always wanted to see what was back there,
cats hair and licorice sticks.

The lent inside my bellybutton
smells something like gasoline.
I light myself on fire,
burn and watch the ashes rise
I get high.
The sky finds a place for me.
We'll wait and see
when the fire department arrives
to put me out.

Lazy Zen Poem 5

If you measure your self worth
by what you own
you're already broke.

Some Pussy And A Poem

I remember getting props
on the pussy I got
even though I didn't
have it at the time
and when I did
have it, I
didn't act like
it was mine.

I remember writing
a scratching the
surface poem that
had potential
to be introspective
but it came off
like a shit to
do list. I haven't
gone back to that
poem yet.

Any Town In America

Sirens whispering in the distance
Freight trains sipping steam
Taggers committing misdemeanors
Painting a piece of life
On the side of a steel machine
Barbed wire surrounding
Elementary school's playground
Basketball goals with no rims
Half full above ground pools
Cops, lots of them
Lingerie shops

Rusty railroad tracks
Still run from one end
Of Podunk out to the city
Limits of Bumfuck.

North Carolina Leaves

Lay on your back
in the mountains of North Carolina
and watch the five o clock
sun reflect off of the oak tree leaves.

Ruffle ruffle from the treetops.

The sounds of the river drift within.

Yum Yum

Our souls dance with romance
and fire crackers blast confetti.
It reminds me of cake
with holes poked in it
and Jell-O is poured into
all the holes
and when the cake is eaten
the tongue can't tell
the difference between
cake and jell-o
and it's all yum yum.

Waiting On A Storm To Come

I sit smoking
sipping tea
waiting on a storm.

Dark clouds hide
the stars.

Steady winds
ruffle leaves
and it sounds
like a stream.

Crickets tweet.
Thunder crumbles.
Flashes of lightning
flicker then
combine to illuminate
the lake.

Fireflies dance
in the distance.

Frogs find friends.
Call and response.

The lake lights up again.
The trees above me
quiet down.

And I decide to roll another
smoke.
Thunder rolls behind me.

The night is quiet.
Only nature speaks.
I get up to get some more tea.

I sit smoking
waiting on the storm to come.

High pitch of a gnat's wing
sings in my eardrums.
I can hear my heartbeat.
I sip my tea.

More frogs are talking.
Now, the stream of tree leaves
ceases for the moment.

Perched birds chirp.
The old rocking chair I'm sitting in
creeks.

The storm has passed
and I never got
to see the rain.

The Sun Rise Crew At A Beach House

It's 4:20
Time to go to bed-
Take the couch-

Party of drunk beach
Spring breakers

Sun is going to shine
Shortly

Hot sand

Shower, pass out
Pass out, shower
Devour- festivities

Enjoy

The world is your
Caught crab dipped in butter
And your Dairy Queen hamburger

Sticky hardwood floors
And drunk Jenga

Old friends
New friends
Good people

Discussing habits
Indulging in whatever
The whim will have

Whatever the mood swings
The mind thinks
Of what to do
And the quickest
Easiest reaction
Is choosed

People wake up for their second wind
The sunrise crew
Jokes
Good folks
Casual cursing

Pop the top
But save those tabs for Ben
Where's the alcohol?!
Take a shot.

Food Poisoning On The Way To New Orleans

We left Greenville at about midnight
to go to New Orleans.
As I drove I remember thinking
I should have hung around a little longer
just to pet my cats and chill with my parents.

I came from Charleston earlier
and luckily I picked up my teammate Kevin
in Greenville so he could drive some.

If you add it all up I was in my
car for almost sixteen hours that day.

About forty miles outside of Atlanta
I got a quezzy NO feeling in my stomach.
I grabbed a paper grocery bag
from the back seat.

Rain came down in sheets.

My eyes teared up.
My mouth got spitty.
Then I heaved.
I heaved my bellybutton
through my esophagus.
I heaved four good times.
I felt the puke on my thighs.
It dripped on my CD case
and on my pants.

Vomit spewed out of my nose.
"Pull over," I said.

The car slowed down.
Vomit was leaking out of
the paper grocery bag at a faster rate.
"Pull over," I said again.
Finally the car came
to a halt under a bridge
in bumper to bumper traffic
on 85.

I flung the door open.
The pounding rain squashed me.
I let one last gust of goo
out of my belly on the soggy
roadside.

Then I dry heaved out of
muscle convulsion until
absolutely everything
was completely out of me.

The last two spurts were
hot and acidic.

I changed pants in the rain
because the ones
I had on were soiled.
I put the soiled pants in the trunk
and got back in the car.

I wiped red gravy off my arms.

From then on
I had the runs about every
sixty miles unless
I was asleep.

Lazy Zen Poem 5

A frayed knot and a stray cable
met in a bar and they both got tore up.

Nothing But A Condom And My Socks On

Swinging my cock
with nothing but a condom
and my socks on.

Hopping on some lockjaw cunt.

On a job hunt.

Slapping my horny
Employee
Balls against a boss snatch.

Waxing a plump rump
Spearing the junk in the trunk
Hearing the moans and groans.

My bone is stone.

Whimpering my damn self.
My penile appendage
is bout
to come lumps of cement semen.

Swinging my cock
Knocking the box
out the park.

Swinging my cock
with nothing but a condom
and my socks on.

Lunch at Crunch Time

at crunch time
I munch mine
in private
in silence
my time
is spent
effectively
efficiently
and wisely.

I scribble and nibble
red pen sandwiches
on text book bread
with computer chips.

My flash cards starve for attention.
I ask tem if they got the memo
and tell them the syllabus is tentative.

I end my lunch break
precisely at 2:30
with a crumb cake
covered in adderal icing.
I sip a Ritalin smoothie.

Motorcycle Accident

Rusty just got in a motorcycle accident.
His brain is swelling.
He wasn't wearing a helmet.
His head hit a car at high speed.
Life is precious.
Life is worthless
if that's how fast disaster
can maim a childhood friend.
I saw him over Thanksgiving
and I remember thinking,
I'll see you in Charleston.
But I don't know how to see you like this.
I didn't want to see you in the hospital.
I wanted to see you in your house
with a smile on your face playing the drums.
I don't know if you can smile right now.
Right now I don't know how to smile.
I want to see you in the brick house
next to mine, jumping on a trampoline.
I want to see you riding a scooter.
You wanted to see you riding a motorcycle.
Helmets don't look cool. Accidents happen
and now look at you, no, I don't want to.
I don't want to see you like this.
I hope medicine or God intervenes.
You'll be ok.
You'll be ok.
You'll be ok.

Lazy Zen Poem 6

If you turned Tiger Woods upside down
would he be sponsored by Newport?

A Gold Digger's Ecstasy

This is a ballad about
the gold digger route.

You better tranquilize
those bank filled eyes.
It's a shame the dame was found
with about a pound of down feathers
in her nostrils.
The skank still rides
Hank till he cries
Stop!
I'm about to drop.

Cops surround the town
like it was a cellblock.
When the hell is the selling going to stop?

When they stop telling her she's hot.
She got tired of being not hired
and fired shots. Screams heard
on the disturbed scene when shots fired.
A perverse scheme has
got dreams deferred.
Like Langston Hughes all I
wanted to do was write.

I fear it's more than cocaine lines
that makes this hoe's brain lame
and die. It's the years of a grinded mind,
grinded by finding the time for stolen rolls,
blinded by buying the kind of drugs that run her life.
Somebody lick her and give her the dick first.

I think she blank blacked out.
Skank drank liquor quicker than
Ben Hur on a chariot.
When he bent her she was very wet.
I'll bet the heroine has yet to take effect.
She wears a neck brace
cause her neck breaks
easily from eating weenie.

The skeeze is teasing him
till the E eases in
and she gives into him.

Just Another Puppet

OK this shit is fucked up.
There is a level of tension here
that is totally unnecessary.
I'm scared of where I'm going
I dared to care and now
I share my very existence.

Dare me to kiss a princess.
Where are we?
Missing a misses when you're with
the very person you turn on?

Burn on herb.

Who's the worst one?

That's absurd.

I got new curse words
I haven't heard before,
curse words you should ignore
because you can't hear them.

We used to adore us.
Trust is stupid if it's blind.
What's the future this time?

The dust that I leave behind
collects and develops into a shadow,
a black whole
a fat whore

Whose got insults?!

Define them while I
underline them.

When its time to sleep
we fumble to slumber.

Did she drink wine on the weekend?
It depends. Was it with family or friends?
Well I don't know.
With kin or a hamlet tease?
OUUU! Pass me the can of peas.
GOO! GOO! Give me the ham and cheese.

Or fruity loops by Toucan Sam and his man, the Jolly Green Giant standing by the tree. While you're at it, ask Janky what he needs. Oh, that danky with no seeds. Some mo hanky panky please and thanks for limbering the lanky into the stanky. And she replies, no, thank me. Beginning sentences with apologies, they start with, I'm sorry, followed by a hollowed vibe of probably, maybe, if you're lucky.

If you're lucky.
If you're lucky.
If you're lucky.

Find another motherfucking puppet.

Questions

Some might call the nightfall a
blanket.

If you are looking for light and you can't
find it.

Gaze straight at the moon
to view a conclusion to your confusion.
Park the car and stare
at the stars far off.

It's hard enough to be where you are
and see all angles realistically.

Angles are tangled with invented intentions.

For instance your existence is split
in divisions of sleeping and rising.

Breathing is comprised of a timeless mindset
to find what life meant.

Was it right or wrong?
Should I fight tonight or be calm
and sleep on it?
Stay or go?
Hold and wait or be bold and race?
Youth or wise?
Truth or lies?
Play or work?
Serious or humorous?
Smoke dope or sober?

Think or drink?
Strive now or lie down?
Thrive on sound?
Or cover your ears to a lover's fears?

To Private 3rd Class With Love

All I saw was an empty bottle of sleeping pills.

Phone off the hook,
streaks of blood on the cheap hotel room wall.

She whispered but I heard a scream
She whispered but I heard a scream

She whispered I don't want to be
human anymore.

It's not about pain
It's not about pain

You could throw me on the concrete
kick me in the teeth
and I wouldn't care
I can't even feel pain.

I didn't know what to say.
All I could come up with was
I would never do that to you.
The world isn't that cruel.
You got a lot going for you
look at you, you're beautiful.

All I could see was an empty bottle
of cheap vodka
next to a note written on a napkin
I couldn't bring myself to read.
I couldn't see her huge pupils
too loopy to fight for life.

She used a 4-½ inch steak knife
and sliced her wrists
to bits and I couldn't see it.
Her pale complexion contrasted
the nine pint glasses of red wine spilled
and smeared.
I couldn't hear her final sigh.
I couldn't feel her heart rate
race at a hundred and 38 beats per minute.
I couldn't believe it.
Her difficulty in breathing became sweet serenity.
I wasn't even there
when Sarah dared to dance
with the dead on the day of reckoning.

So let the angels sing

Cease the heartbeat lord
That keeps my soul captive
Let my story be told
When the sole trumpet blows that somber song of taps
At dusk
Ashes to ashes
I love you much
Drift away
Drift away

I Wish I Would Shut Up

I keep you locked in a box
so the world does not see you.
I keep you so confused
you don't even want to be you.
I degrade you.
The only way for you to see
is through me
Your eyes are mine.
I am your mind.

You're crying one minute
and laughing the next.
Riding the sky like waves
and then crashing like hard drives.
You nose dive so low
you thought you died.
As long as you've been alive
you fly solo.
Nobody has the patience
to deal with your craziness.

You live in a torture chamber.
Pouring your pain and anger
into pages from pens.
You're thin. You don't eat for days.
You're transparent. I can see through your skin.

As a child you just thought
you were strange.
Growing up you realized
you were insane.
When you answered to the voices
That were calling out your name.

So you were diagnosed
with a few slight disorders.
Agoraphobia, paranoia, bi polar
you feel blindfolded. Burnt, scolded and alone
like nobody cares for you.

You stay in bed for days
cause you stay distressed.
I am the covers that you are under.
I am the thunder cracks and lighting bolts.
I am the frightening jolts
That shock through you
when you have a panic attack.

When you look in the mirror
and look back at me
you see that we
are the gruesome reality that attacks sanity
and gives its lacerations.
No amount of bandages
can handle these damn damages.
Just when you think you can't stand it
I'll take what's left
until you pray for death.
So stay depressed you crazy mess.

Some say you lost your mind
but you and I know the truth.
I'm right here with you.

Isolation, fuck it.
Sensory depravation, in public.
Black out without passing out.
Loss of consciousness only to wake up
vomiting promises
to the outside world and to your girl

about how you're going to change.
That's a damn shame.
You and I know you're going remain the same.

Cross eyed slugs bathing in sea salt
singing hymns of praise to silence.

Cross eyed slugs bathing in sea salt
singing hymns of praise to silence.

Shake the rape of your imagination

You're a machine, an assembly line
a fiend of your own mind.

I'm never letting you go.

Tribute To Poets

This is for all those who
keep it locked, cocked and loaded
ready to explode with a flow
of trophy poetry flowing free.
This is for hip hop.
This is for spiritual lyricists, rhymers and freestylers.
This is for writers of prose and journalism,
learning the trade of the pen to the page.
This is for the weed smokers who need focus.
This is for Jack Kerouac, Sapphire and Langston Hughes.
This is for those
searching for the truest form of communication
willing to go against the norm with spoken word.
This is for attentive eyes listening
to attentive ears listening.
This for anybody who can spit shit.
This is for the kid who locked himself in his room,
staring at the walls caused he's pissed at his parents
breaking pencil after pencil
until he thinks of the right word to write.
This is for any man that can close his eyes
hold a mic, and let his ideas to take flight
and for everyone who feels at home when they rhyme.
This is for two one liners and haikus.
This is for true artist working
harder and harder to find truth.
This is for the volume never turned down
on a rhythmic heart.
This is for the host who keeps it moving swift,
The poet who never quits doing it
and the crowd that keeps on moving with
every wind swooshed up off the stage.
This is for everybody that has something to say.

Words of Wisdom That Didn't Come Out Right

An older brother says to his younger brother,
"There are only
three people in this
world,
the one who makes it happen
the one who watches it happen
and the one who says, 'what happened?'"

The younger brother replies, "If that is so
I have already fucked myself, because I
know I have fucked more than three people."

Ben

Allison just called me and told me Ben was a wreck.

In family photos me and Ben always stood next to each other.
In real life we were closer than that.
The only thing that ever came between us was women.

But our habits changed, our lives changed.

He moved, then I moved away from home.

Mom and dad gave us freedom and hoped we had enough momentum to make it.
Mom was quiet. Dad was loud.

Both of them were proud of us at certain times in our childhood.

Sometimes we didn't see it.
Sometimes he didn't see it.

Growing up, we were always in the thick of it together and we shared each other's emotions.

When I went away to college I had a girlfriend and me and her shared emotions more than me and Ben used to.
When she wasn't there for me I felt totally alone and part of that was because me and Ben weren't as close.

After a while I picked up my shit. I picked up my life and I decided that I would carry my emotions by my damn self. Along my journey a little while ago I wondered where Ben's emotions were. I wondered if he was carrying them.

I remember at the end of my freshman year when I couldn't hold myself up on my own two feet and all I wanted to do was lay in bed all day long. I called Ben and told him that I lost it and I wasn't able to hold on anymore.

He said, "What do you mean?"

"I mean I couldn't- I just- I lost it man- everything- nothing made sense anymore and I lost it."

He said, "You mean like crying?"

I said, "Yeah but I couldn't turn it off."

He said, "Yeah I've done that too man."

I wish Ben would call me right now.

Car Wreck

I write in the corner table at 12:34 at night in the Waffle House.
    I drank too much to drive and my house is down Woodruff,
    right at highway 14, and left into Holly Tree.
My memory follows me on the ride home. I close my eyes, take
    a drag and hiss like a cat. I pull a longer puff of nicotine
    and exhale my blood stream as bright as the headlights.
    The cold stings as I stroll to the car. Holding my pen like
    a cigar, I
fall on my way to the car like Holden Claufield but I feel no
    pain.

Sobriety hits me like a blue light flashing.

I tell my subconscious it's not honest, it must be lying to me.
    Drivers speed by, smoke rises from my dying cigarette.
    And I know that tomorrow will be another day.

I stay in the corner and look to my right, I see the reflection of
    me in the glass. I am slow.
I am older than I remember myself. I remember when I was
    sixteen and I could drive by myself at night for the first
    time. I was driving down Augusta today. When I crossed
    Byrd Street I thought about prom night in my mom's Q45.

Taking a left at a green light that I thought was an arrow
a bronco t-boned me and I slid halfway sideways.
I floored the foot pedal to the floorboard. Panicked,
"Damn it!" were the first words that I uttered. I
shuttered at the thought of jail time. Up the hill
in time to get out of the sight of the headlights behind me.
Took my first right, drove about a hundred feet, parked
On the street, and turned my headlights off before
the Bronco sped off behind me.

On The Third Shelf

I ordered a number two with onion rings instead of fries. I waited patiently next to all the other fat people. All I could hear in the background was fat people munching on burgers and fries. I always get fries. I'm sick of fries. I want something different. I need to change. Bobby, I know his name is Bobby because of his red and gold nametag, - Bobby handed me my super sized number two and the see through bag dripped with grease. His face was full of pimples. I waddled over to the plastic table in the corner and with contempt I grinded my teeth upon burnt onion rings and listened to a baby cry at the other end of the restaurant. My dad keeps his gun behind some books wrapped in a blue rag on the third shelf of the bookcase in his bedroom.

The Phone Doesn't Ring Much Anymore

he looks at love as just a memory.
empty ashtrays fill his days.
misery is all he sees.
he'd call his friends but they told him off.
he'd call his family but they wrote him off.
another half ass writer coughs in his hand
in the window of a coffee shop.

he smiles at the thought of sleep.
he dreams of getting his life back together.
it's like a puzzle missing the pieces.
his troubles are drank away on the weekend.
he reads another bukowski short story and
instead of writing a poem he slacks off and jacks off
and thinks about the first girlfriend he ever had.

the phone doesn't ring much anymore.
the bills are piling up.
the windowsills are coated with dust.
his stomach still churns from
throwing up last night.

to pass the time he lays in bed
and debates the fastest
easiest solution to fix his problems.
he gets bothered at the thought of effort.

he consciously tells himself
that the best years of his life are gone.
once again he spends another
calm night fet up and in tears piercing
the boredom with stiff liquor drinks.

he thinks how did he come so far
but not really get anywhere.

Exams

I'm going to get drunk
or maybe take a nap when this is over.
I can't wait to take a break
from all of this studying.

These tests stress me out
to the point that I doubt if it's all worth it.

I guess it's worth it.

Because if it wasn't
I'd be getting drunk or taking a nap.

Fake

I remember the day
I fell in love with her
on the other side
of a one way mirror.

She removed her crystal cat eyes
and gave them to me
but I knew she wasn't watching.

I peered deep into her deep sockets.

I could taste yesterday's smoke
in my lungs on the day of her wake.
I woke up
hung over, drunk and sober all the same.

When I arrived at the church
I dropped a candy bar in the collection plate.

The preacher pulled a rabbit out of a hat
and some chicken blood
and pig's feet out of the deceased.

She wasn't really dead.
She wasn't ever watching.
And I already fucked somebody else anyway.

Lazy Zen Poem 7

If you judge your self worth by what you own
you are already broke.

A Moment Of Silence

Before I begin this poem
I would like to have a moment of silence
I would like to have a moment of silence
For the time spent waiting and wondering
I would like to have a moment of silence
For all who have lost their way
And all those that gave up before they got started
And for every white picket fence that never got built
And for the all the households
In which 2.5 children were aborted
I would like to have a moment of silence
For every kid that never made the team
For every one who has heard, time out, I need time alone
For every tear that fell on deaf ears
For anybody that thought they weren't good enough
I would like to have a moment of silence
For the violence that occurred in retaliation after 911
For the racist slurs that were made towards Islamic people
For the hateful words that were uttered
out of every ignorant bloodthirsty American
I would like to have a moment of silence
For the eighteen year old kid who is about to die
In the upcoming war
Hey fuck it at least Billy got a flag across his coffin
They sent him home in a box like he was chocolate
I would like to have a moment of silence
For anybody who gave up
to save what
they still had
For every dad that beats his child
And for every mother
who shutters when she watched it

happen but was too frozen to stop it
I would like to have a moment of silence
For every for every freshman girl
who got touched by the staff of La Hacienda
after free margaritas while she was passed out

I would like to have a moment of silence

Follow The Person In Front Of You

A call for revolution falls short
because we resort
to the most comfortable option.
Almost effortlessly
I follow the carrot
held in front of my nose.

This carrot is beer,
this turtle here
is a card carrying carrot follower.

These are not your Wal-Mart carrots
even though they do have lower prices.

These are name brand carrots.
This is a polo carrot.
And if I could lick the sweat off the 12 year old
who made my pants, I wouldn't.
If I could look at
the twelve-year-old who made my pants
I wouldn't.

If I could boycott
all the problem perpetuating products
I probably wouldn't.
Because I like to be spoon-fed my culture.

I would describe myself as a vulture
swooping down to buy what everybody else got.

So I can look fresh and new and hot.
I'll proudly display the label
so you know how much it costs.

Give me a moment of silence
for looking cool.
Give me a moment of silence
for fitting in.
Give me a moment of silence
for not going against the grain.

I couldn't swim up stream if I wanted to.
The movement of current events is too quick.

If I were a newspaper
I'd jack off my constituents for money.
If I were a whore
I'd be the most honest person in this room.
If I were a catholic priest
I'd tell the congregation to follow Buddha.

If I were a revolutionary
I'd sit on my ass and talk about it.

Everybody wants to be down.
Everybody wants to be in the click.
Even not being pretty
is being down with the ugly kids,
hence gothic, hot topic, dungeons and dragons and
The kids that scream loudly
"yeah I'm a faggot, poser!" proudly.

Feed the beast.
Silence yourself

So wear your goddamn name brand.
Drink your Coca-cola.
Go to Disney world.
It's the American way.

And don't vote, the election is wrigged anyway
but if you do vote
vote for the white guy
who wants to bring back the draft.
Vote for the white guy
who thinks public education should be cut short
because our military needs longer guns.

You could refer to him as *the man*
or *the establishment* or even better
as every Gill Scott look alike
likes to refer to him, as *whitey*
Or *the white man.*
No, I'll make it easier

It's me.

I am the white guy
who has been killing Native Americans
and oppressing every other non-Arian race
since this great country started.

I look for you vote in 2004.

A Revolution Televised

Gill Scott was many things
But most importantly
Gill Scott was wrong.
The revolution will be televised.

You are tuned in to the march.
You rally on the capital
Every time you watch the news.

I got news.
I am not afraid.
I do not lock my door.
I do not own a television.

If you lock your door at night
You perpetuate the fear
That someone will come into your home
And do harm to you and your family.

If you have been watching the news you know
That the suspect to watch out for is
A 6 foot 2 black male wearing baggy jeans
Timberland boots and racing jacket.

Hey, but the news isn't all bad.
Put your 2 year old in front of the TV.
See, he stops crying.
Look how big his eyes get.
He is memorized.
He is hypnotized.
He is brainwashed.
Wash the stains of imagination off.

Scrub the creativity out of your child's young mind.
The revolution is being televised.

The revolution is about money.
It is about fear.
It is about ignorance.
Where else are you going to get your low self esteem.
How are you going to know
Which new car you want to lease.

Don't you want to be fat?
Wait, you are fat.
You watched so many Burger King commercials
You turned into a regular there.
They promote free choice.
You just want to have it your way.

The revolution is televised.
You just bought into it.
Colgate told you your teeth were yellow.

You will get laid off if you drink beer.
You will get laid if you drink beer.
Drink responsibly.
Binge drinking is bad.
Binge drinking is the bread and butter
Of beer companies.

Did the make up commercial remind you
you were ugly?

Did the news pump enough fear into you yet?
Maybe you were able to resist it.
Maybe you are not scared.
But you are distracted
And that is what the revolution is all about.

It is designed to keep you stupid.
It is designed to keep you consuming.
You can't change the government don't even try.

I had a dream where Bush
And Cheney were at a gas station.

They were pumping grade 93 gas all over each other.
They were naked accept for
Orange blow up floaties around there biceps.
They had a kkk hoods on
And written across both of their chests was a message.
It said WE ARE ROBOTS.
The black gold sponged slimy on their skin
Like it was amniotic fluid.
The gas station attendant came outside
And lit them on fire.
He was a black man charged with
Lighting the vice president
And president of the United States
On fire while being black.

Cheney performed porn movie quality fellatio on Bush.
Bush came oil as he burned in flames.

I woke up to the sounds of gunfire.
Another man shot his child.
His sixteen year old kid snuck out to smoke pot
In the early hours of the morning.
When he crept back in
His father, Charlton Heston, turned on the light.
He then looked at his own flesh and blood
And fired three rounds into the back of his own child.
While screaming, "FROM MY COLD DEAD HANDS."
That child was the American people's since of security.
Charlton Heston pulled a Susan Smith
And blamed it on a black guy.
The cycle continues.

The evening news reported the story
And there you have it, a revolution televised.
This revolution is designed to keep you fat
Racist, ignorant and scared.
Most importantly
This revolution is designed
To keep you the red blooded American that you are.

Give And Take

In a society of givers and takers
you could lie to me
and say you were neither
a generator or a drainer.

But the truth of the matter
is even if you remain passive and silent
you are adding to the silence
or subtracting from the noise.

Energy is constantly in flux.
Love is the transfer of positive energy.

Sometimes you must talk and listen
with just eye contact.

givers and takers
those who live it and fakers
generators and drainers
pimps and hoes

Honkey Pimps

I'm smoking pot by my damn self
and no thank you, I don't need any help.
Keep talking while I'm already walking away.
You're always waiting on me
to finish what I'm saying.
Sentences never ending and never ending sentences.
You bet I'll smoke your last cigarette
and tell you to get more
when you go to the store.

Honkey pimps riding donkeys with limps
drinking long island ice tea might be
the only people who can see me right now.
Bitch is iced out with semen on her titties
in her belly button and her smelly butt.
She's got hickies on her hips.
I got bite marks on my dick.
I'm sparking fights with farting dykes tonight.

Gluttony

rank pussy stank goodly enough
but what I am search for is
cigarettes, beer and fried food.

you can find you salvation in a happy meal,
liberation in a six pack.
you can handle life within a box of camel lights.
it's fun to fuck your lungs and tell your liver to shut up.
rise your gluttony to an entire higher level.

bean burritos, baby food, and prunes.
keep your colon clean.
take a shit for the team.
break wind if you know what I mean.

Ignorant Virgin

Good evening
Good riddance
Good night

Question my ideals with your ignorant logic.
Call me powerless and fearful
But I will not retaliate

I am by nature an impartial observer
So blow your top
Go nuts
Lose your temper
And you get even more pissed when I don't retaliate
You wish I would snap back
But I laugh at that

Have some fucking respect
Have some class
Have some dick but not from me
I'm not taking the V-card retard

Question my ideals then you leave pissed
You said, "don't talk to me
Unless you have something good to say"
Well I don't, not for you, so piss off
Take your uppity bitch attitude and go away

Learn to drink and think before you speak
Please
I'm not affected
Selected emotions stay hidden
I never kissed you so forever I will never miss you

You show your true colors and you're ugly
Hey, and I am too
Diamond in the ruff, allow me to contradict myself

What the fuck does a virgin know about sex

After A Late Night In London

I got a crazy virgin shitting on me
I got a gay guy hitting on me

And besides this I got her sidekick
A lady with a lazy eye trying to fade me,
Right?

It's seven-o clock and I'm still trying to
fucking recover from last night

I was butter past nine
I was bent at ten
Devilish at eleven
And hell at twelve

For god sakes, I've been awake for three hours today

I need a shower right away

Last night
I smoked weed and peed on the streets

Lazy Zen Poem 9

Last night I took a shit on a toilet that was so nasty
I put a condom on before I sat down.

Imagine A Nation

imagine a nation
facing breaks within the ranks of organization.
it traces history back to its most recent news station.

use your imagination
ask yourself if the wealth of a nation
depends on men who seat in seats.
these men depend on what the other man is thinking.

it's a groupthink:
an exercise in how many guys
can think the same thing
and then talk to a bunch
of other guys who think the same thing.

except, the first group is ruined by a speech they got
about how their balls were bigger.
the ball size was determined by their leader.
he was a cheater
stealing oil and spoils from the nation
that he beat.

it all competes with Greek Mythology.
these are times new roman.
through hocus pocus and hypnotists
geniuses calculate
the distance between nuclear warfare
and spookier dookie
like the group think thinking that royal imperialism
is better than any other option.

I hear adoption rates

are really good on the 51'st state.
colonize at Stalin speed
quicker than bees around honey.

burn
pillage
contract
track resources

forces use unreasonable force
to build walls around fortresses.
the moat is a goat eating a boot.

stupidity is more effective than tear gas
and much more wide spread than mustard gas.

perhaps, that's why pretentiousness
is deemed commendable among businessmen.

because it's better
to look like you know what you're talking about
than to go out on a ledge and know the difference.

that's why the radicals
are seen as unbelievable and drastic
because they are asking
for a piece of your undivided attention.

use your imagination to picture a nation
that thrives on vegetation as much as herbivores do
except this time
the vegetarian is very into the natural resources
of other countries

and its bread is the led that is fed to the draft age

twenty somethings wanting
something more than stories of glory

who's going to fight for you?
who's going to risk their life
to watch the rest of the world decline
for the respect and acceptance
of the great imagined nation.

Dear Allison

Allison you're challenging.
You're a pal and friend.

And more than now and again,
I glance across the room
And wonder, "Who is this loon?"

Who could be so smooth
And so clumsy and so sexy,
All in the same second?

Who could have
A sense of humor drier than a desert
And eyes cuter than a baby's?

Well it's that lady that
Walks with the confidence of a brick
And the calm defense of knowing it's all right.

All night you're as cool as a cucumber
And as fun as a juggling jester
And as relaxed as a cat
And as bouncy as a basketball
And as down to earth as dirt
And as bright as fire.

Allison, you're the coolest ice cube in the tray
And the hottest ray from the sun
And the one that comes to mind
Because we always have a good time.

Pensively yours,
 Love,
  Jonathan Brown

Do You Believe In Monogamy?

A nympho goes low and blows
a man in a tuxedo in the back of a limo.
A massive load is blown
and mayo flows slowly like molasses.
Floodgates dilate and nuts deflate.
Fellatio is great but she's still got a date with a
third rate vibrator.
Why date her?

Skyscrapers stand tall.
He views the moon
through the moon roof.
Through the blackness he notices aurora borealis.
He pops in a juicy fruit chew
and chews.
Then he empties the tobacco from a Philly Blunt
pulls out a bag full of cannabis
mumbles something about getting damn blitzed
and rolls a jumbo potato
while he tells this ho about how she met the status quo

"Bravo! Bravo!
Bitch, haven't I seen you in a porno flick?
I hope this isn't hubris
but you miss,
define why
children still fly kites."

He lights the blunt
waves it around and says,

"That was as fun

as watching some
gun fight on the TV show Sopranos.
Thank you for the hanky panky.
I appreciate you spanking me.
You even drank the spooge I spewed
without even using a tissue.
I admit when I farted it sounded
like a didgeridoo
but it was long overdue.
I've been holding the gas
Since my wife blue balled me"

Lazy Zen Poem 10

My dick is so small
I piss on my balls.

Cory

I'm going to tell a story
about a sly guy named Cory.

Cory was never boring
but when Cory was horny
he would go to the store for cheese
snort speed of the floor
puff weed with whores
and huff paint indoors.

He stained his draws
when he pissed his pants.
He would walk around town
with shit in his hands.
He would go and throw
logs of poo poo at people
doo doo again
and come back for a sequel.

He would scream mean things
while riding his bike at night
like, "I'm going to kill you!"

His pupils were huge from pills that he'd do.
He was a tragic drug addict
with a habit of making love to fucking faggots
He'd sell his ass crack for crack fast.
I heard he sucked dick for drugs and shit

This sick fuck,
I saw him licking some fired up retired white guys nuts
with a pair of pliers in his butt.

It was nasty.
My eyes closed tight shut.

3 hookers

I recall when I was in a Holiday Inn with my balls in hand. My limp penis pointed at three coked up, so fucked hookers. Me and the ghost of Elvis Pressley were five way sexing these three satisfied ladies of the night. Nasty thighs, track marks, cum puddles and speed bumps were worn like badges of honor.

For some reason nobody felt bad.

Nancy's noo noo was spread wide open like the opening of a bread bag that draped over a kitchen table. Nancy was into fisting. So the pleasure in that hole was not all gravy but what a novelty item. The Polaroid's prove it.

Eve's thing was boofooing from behind combined with autoeroticafixiation. I am no stranger to the butt but when she wanted me strangle her with a wet shoelace I thought it was a little much. I wondered how she started this technique. I tried to picture her masturbating in her parent's bathroom, her box in one hand, and her throat in the other. But I just couldn't do it. This practice of hers must have been learned from someone else. She probably searched far and wide to find the correct mentor to study under.

Molly's oddity was that she loved golden showers. And I don't know why they call it a golden shower. I mean, it's not like anyone is getting clean during this process. The biggest problem with golden showers is that they are contagious. After I peed on Molly, Eve and Nancy wanted me to pee on them too. Sure I had Jack Daniel's flowing through me like a river but what do you do when you're out of pee? I told those hookers to go in the bathroom so the bed wouldn't stink and move the blow up doll out of the way if they wanted to pee on each other.

Pee stinks and I'm not sure but I think Nancy plopped a log on Molly too because Nancy had a skid mark towards the bottom of her bread bag.

The ghost of Elvis was content playing riffs on his guitar in the corner after the hookers were asleep. I just stayed up and watched C Span with my irritated balls in my hand.

Lazy Zen Poem 11

My dick was acting up
so I had to beat it down.

Dark At A Young Age

Let's get this straight
I don't owe you shit

I'd hate for you to get confused
I won't be very amused
I've been boozed for days
Living in a haze, tripping
Over my own feet in this maze

Slower to sleep
Lying awake shaking
Contemplating fate
My destiny's going to get
The best of me
Look at me
Can you see the crook in me?
I could sell drugs

Look at me
Can you see the other side of me?
I plan to be erased
I'm sorry for everyone that's cried for me

I'm chased by a man with a gun
Loaded with pain
The bullet is made of the same lame shit
That made me cry when I was little
My memories are going to pull it
Ending me

I'm having nightmares
Sitting right here

Fighting years past
Frightened tears last
Time
I had that on my mind
I felt blind
I couldn't see what
Was in front of me
I can't walk
And I can't talk
Because I'm caught up
I'm going to get shot up
By my memories
Ending me
Sending me to place
I don't want to go

Memories of my face
Being bruised and battered
My tooth shattered
When he hit me
He knocked the shit out of me
But I was so plastered
I didn't feel it
Isn't that some real shit?

The cousin to my anger
Is when I feel stranger
Like I'm in danger
There is a killer following me
Insecurity is worse
Than being dead
The walls are coated with bloodshed
Like someone's head exploded and
Their brains are falling apart

But the halls of my head
Are filled with the tall

Thoughts of being bought
And being caught up in
Something I can't handle
So I light a candle

And think of my memories
Ending me
Rendering me a paraplegic
And I'm blind so I don't care
If I can't see shit

You'll never be shit
When are you going to see it?
That you're a fuck up
Your lucks up
Nobody wants to hear you speak
So shut up

But I got feet
And I can walk away
From anybody that
Talks to me that way
Outlines of chalk around me
My chest is blown in
But I guess while I'm here
I'll count mine, and realize that
Everything is a blessing
And in this life, I got
One chance to do it right

The nights will end
The days will begin
And I'll do the best that I can
Up until the end

I Drove Past Your House

I drove past your house
because I was thinking about
how you've been doing.

I got somebody new
and I know you do to
but
I miss the way it was
impossible to resist your kiss.

Is this thought a shot in the dark
or do the sparks in your heart still exist?
You ignited a flame
that can never be extinguished.

Through the fights and the pain
and the cold nights and the rain
I can close my eyes and go
back in time
and remember the sunshine you shined
once upon a time
upon my life.

When we split I was torn
between the meaning of dreams
and the rationality of reality.

I tried to ration my emotions
but
I finally broke beneath
the pressure of staying together.

You used to kiss me
and say that you wished we
could stay together forever.

I kept driving because I've been riding
with the thought of you for a while
and I figured what was another afternoon
of chasing after you in my mind
but a regular occurrence.

Besides, you're probably over me.
What would it be like
if I stopped by
and we talked for a while?

It might be slightly
uncomfortable for both of us.

In hope I trust we will see each other
at another time in a different light
where we can kick it one night
and not be frightened
by the thought of how
the night might end.

Even though
I might never say these things to you
I daydream of you and me swinging on swings
with ice cream cones in our hands
laughing at how our thumbs
look like small big toes.

Then we'd walk on the battery
and talk of attraction.
The forbidden fruit would be ripe
for picking and soon we would be kissing
and passionately embracing
and cat bathing naked in the fountain.

and shouting and shouting
and screaming and pounding
and creaming and bouncing
and leaping and bounding
and keeping the level of arousal
at a maximum.

We would come and relax
and come and relax
and come and relax and
relax again.

Well anyways,
that's been on my mind.

I hope your doing fine
I say to myself as I drive by.

You Got A Life To Live

You got a life to live baby.
What you sticking around here for?
I thought you'd be long gone years ago
Off to college and out in the workforce
Being a workhorse for a big company
Or starting something of your own.

You got a life to live baby
What you sticking around here for?
Ain't nothing here for you but
Dried tears, misguided careers
And old friends that aren't too friendly anymore
Why don't you get up and get out
There is whole world out there waiting on you.

And she says, "I'm going to save up,
I'm going to save up enough
To get out of this old town."
But ain't nothing here for you

We spend our lives waiting
Waiting for summer time
Waiting for the semester to be over
Waiting to graduate
Waiting for grad school applications
Waiting for job interviews
Waiting for pay day
Waiting for promotions
Waiting for a lunch break

A smoke break
A day that we can rest

A daydream
A phone call
An alarm clock
The hand of God

It's all right here
Baby don't wait
You can waist your life away
If you wait long enough

Tell you what.
Tomorrow let's go down to the funeral home
And pick out a nice mahogany casket
With bronze bars for the pall bearers
To hold onto.
We'll even go down to the flower shop
And pick out a fitting arrangement
We'll plan the whole thing out.
I'll help you write the eulogy
So you can rest easy knowing that
Everything is taken care of
Then you can know what you're waiting for
And next time you get your paycheck
Instead of paying bills
We'll get in the car
And see how far it will take us.

We'll drive until the gaslight comes on
And then we'll stop and get some junk food
Along with some unleaded
Then will get back in the car and
Drive up 95 until it's suitable to go west
Then will drive west until
We need to get gas again
Well stop whenever something looks interesting
We'll stop when our eyes double take.

We'll climb a water tower
We'll sleep in the park
We'll travel until we find what we're looking for

But we can't know what we're looking for before we go
We just got to go

Cancel tomorrow
Forget about all the plans you've made
Set aside all your obligations
And stop waiting for tomorrow to come

We All Fall In Line

You learn survival through surviving.
Keep in mind to keep time in mind.
Your time in this life is limited.
What will they say about you when you're gone?
Live as if the next day may not be completed.
Indeed each of us breaths a finite supply of air.
Care about everything.
Call the ones you love.
Apologize for falling behind.

Because when the time comes
when we all fall in line
and march into mortality
the small things are the things that will matter.
Rather than act average
act as if this is the last time
you will ever see the person in front of you.

Alone

Today I woke up alone.
I ate breakfast alone.
I watched a really fucked up movie alone.
I went for a jog alone.
I did my dishes alone.
I read alone.
I slept alone.
I woke up alone.
I made dinner alone.
I read alone.
I'm writing this, now, alone.

My cat Cummings just sat on my lap.
My cat wants to love me.
My cat wants to be loved.

My cat is satisfied passing time in silence
and I am reminded of why
I love my cat so much.

Lazy Zen Poem 12

Sometimes jacking off and playing
video games are not the best things to do.

The Problem With War

The problem with the war
is that

it can't be sustained.

Most people lighten up after a little while.

Lucky

The passenger side window of my car
was smashed when I came home
two days ago.

I felt lucky like I had won
the lottery.

How many people does that happen
to everyday?

Not many.
Yup.
I sure am special.

Then the dude who fixed the glass
said that a Corolla up the street
had its window smashed in too.

I thought, wow,
I really am special.

I called the police after it happened to
tell them, because it's always fun
to deal to cops under those circumstances.

They arrive faster than pizza.

I got a telephone call from the cops this morning.
They wanted to know if anything was taken.
They asked if I knew who did it.

I felt like I had a pissed off

pit bull by the muzzle
and I could let him loose on anyone.

That Night I Educated Myself

I'll tell you why,
I'll tell you why I got a C+ in my
poetry rhyme and meter class.

Before the first test
I was screaming poetry on a rooftop
in front of a rock band
on the night
of the president's state of the union address.

King Street was flooded with people.
We made a scene.
We had to pack up and dip before the police came.

By the time I ran to Maybank for my class
I was so charged with adrenaline
I couldn't recall my short term memory.

I couldn't regurgitate specific terms.
Definitions eluded my stabbing mind.
The stream of consciousness was flowing too fast
for me to reach down and catch a definition
swimming on the shallow riverbed.

I was on a rooftop living the life.
I was so charged
I blew a fuse running the track meet
to meet academia

But that was a valuable night.

My pops always says

you can have everything you want in this life
just not at the same time

Well I made my decision
and I wouldn't trade it
for a water down version of blaa.

The lessons I learned on the rooftop
go beyond anything English 395
had to offer that day.

I failed the first test
because I was out getting educated.

This Is Not A Good Poem

since I woke up
I've completed
many tasks but
I haven't start-

ed working on
the most import-
ant challenge, which
is to finish

all of my home
work. I haven't
even written
this poem. It's

not a poem
without whores, or
drugs, or God, or
violence, or war,

or sex, or lust,
or shitting and
farting. It's not
a good poem

without nature,
or children, or
pain and heartache,
or addiction,

or smiling
or orgasms

or caskets. Oh
yeah caskets that's

great. Real concrete.
Add specific
names of towns no-
body's ever

heard of and you
can be just like
James Tate. Well I
haven't added

any of that. So
this is not a
good poem. I
am trying to

be as bland as
whiteout sniffers
stiff with rigi-
mortis bound by

Norton

Beautiful Robot

She was a pimp's kryptonite
Her gears grinded tight
Switches switched
Sprockets rocking
Her kiss was dry
Pumping pistons
Pulleys fully extended

But listen
You will hear no heartbeat
Just the tick tock of a clock
Manufactured passion
And cold steel magnetic touch
Synthetic trust
Electric lust
Rust on her neck
And dust on her breast

Shit Happens

we're next to her dad's office downtown
and she says
she has to pee
and her dad's office is right there
so we just go up
to her dad's office

and I'm like, cool.

so she pees
and then I have to take a shit
because we just ate sushi
but it wasn't the kind of sushi
that just sits with you.
it was swimming through me.

when I sit down
I get the runs
and I shit and I shit
and I shit some
extra liquid stuff
I mean I really got the runs.

and I'm pretty sure I'm getting laid
but I'm not sure when
because this chick is freaky
and it could happen at anytime.

so I wipe my ass
and I wipe my ass
and I wipe again
six more times just

to make sure that I do not
have a muddy asshole
before I get some pussy.

so I walk out of the bathroom
all unsuspecting and shit
and she is looking at a picture of duck
in the woods on the wall
and I look at the picture
real close to her
and I hug her from behind
and she grabs my arms
and hugs her with them
and then I kiss her neck
right below her ears
and the next thing I know
her tongue is down my throat
and I'm all cool with it
because I wanted to hump
and I was pretty sure
I was gonna hump
so I had some
condoms in my pocket.

so things get a little freaky
and we get down to business.

and she's on top
and I'm sitting up
with my back leaned against
an antique white couch
and we're doing it
I mean we are really riding
she is getting so deep
she's all the way down
to the end of my dick.
my pubes are all soaked

and she is about to cum
so she is all gyrating
and throwing
extra motions in the mix
and she's riding me good.

and I'm rubbing
my naked butt against
this white antique couch.

and it was really good sex.

so after I blow my jizz
all up against
the inside of a Trojan
she's got to pee
so she goes to the bathroom
and I stand up
and I get ready to go to the bathroom
and take this fucking rubber
off my shlong
and I look down
at the white
antique couch
and I guess

I didn't wipe my ass
properly because
there is a big
SKIDMARK
on the white antique couch
in her dad's office.

so when she got
out of the bathroom

I got in the bathroom

and I flushed the rubber
down the toilet.

when I came out of the bathroom
she had her cloths on
and I put mine on

and before we left
I took one last look
at that shit stain
on the white antique couch.

W

Osoma Bin Laden's
been hiding at my ranch in Texas.
I've been supplying
his camp with the weapons.

When I didn't pay out
he blew up two buildings.
When he was hiding out
I bombed civilians.

I'll convince the nation to commence racism
against men in turbans with skin
about as brown as bourbon.

While the younger generation laughs at the draft
Sanford signs his resignation to return to the reserves.

I'll drain the everglades
and sniff cocaine
and rig the next election
like I did the last.

Waffle Prose

It was a normal day just as any other. Nothing to different about the scene. The smoke was stale. The coffee was cold. The staff was bitching about who was doing dishes. There was a new waitress named Jill. Jill was a nineteen year old winy girl. She learned it as a baby. You cry, you get what you want, so, she cried. And boy could she ever bitch about every little thing imaginable. She'd ask for more hours and then bitch because she didn't have time to have fun. She'd say her throat hurts after she exhaled a Marlboro red. She was certain she didn't have to do anything she didn't want to do. The only problem was she didn't want to do anything. She was screaming at Leroy about how she's gone go and tell Marty what he said to her and that nobody ever talks to her like that. The only problem was that Leroy didn't say anything and Marty doesn't give a shit.

I came in on Saturday night on my way home. I stopped off because I didn't think it was safe for me to be on the rode. I usually set out with the idea that I won't drink too much when I know I have to drive. But sometimes I get ahead of myself and guzzle at gulp pace. So I drank for three straight hours at my friend Preston's house. By this time my tummy was full of beer and I had to pee every fifteen minutes. It was getting about time to pee. It was raining. I hadn't changed my windshield wipers since I got my car four years ago and I've never washed the windshield so when it rained the windshield was illiterate. It looks like you were wearing beer goggles even if you weren't wearing beer goggles and I was wearing beer goggles so it was pretty bad.

So I stop at the Waffle House on Woodruff Road. It was a new one so they had newer booths but it was the same trusty menu. I sought solace and coffee and water and chocolate pie. I wanted to get off the road.

When I walked in the door the Backstreet Boys song "As

Long As You Love Me" was playing over the jukebox. There was a young crooked teethed waitress singing along with the music. She was dancing in her seat at the end of the counter like a belly dancer in a wheelchair.

My first thought was Jesus, fuck, is this bitch going to play shitty music the entire time I'm here. She brought me a cup of coffee and a glass of water. She set out a napkin, fork, knife, and spoon like they always do. She shot me a smile and I lightened up. I pulled out my notebook and looked over some recent poems I wrote. My purpose here was to jam them together so I could have one long poem. I write a lot on the same subject or topic for about a week and then I melt them together where the changes fit and take out the parts that are just empty rhetoric.

I remember one time I went to Waffle House and I walked into the bathroom. There was blood splattered one of the walls. A large handprint smeared the burgundy against the white tile. At first I thought about telling the people that worked there what I had seen. But then I thought that they probably knew about it and they might have had something to do with it. If I let them know that I knew then I would have something to do with it and I didn't want that. I covered my hand with my shirt and pushed the door handle open. I didn't want my fingerprints at the scene of the crime. I got my book bag and left the money on the counter and got the fuck out of there.

Gloria

Brown leaves fall from tall oak trees.
The autumn wind blows briskly.
She will be missed.

This goes out to Gloria.
I was going to take
her to the Peace Center
to see Swing
but she had friends visiting from Virginia
that weekend and she said
she should spend
that evening with them.

So I said cool.
I didn't see her again after our first encounter.
Now I'll never see her.

I keep Gloria in the back left side of my head.
She was the waitress at Sunday brunch
when my whole family was around the table
at the Holly Tree Country Club.
I had tickets to a show in about a week
and I needed a date.

After my family ate we went outside
and we were about to ride back to the house.
My dad pulled his keys from his pocket.
I told my family I'd be right back
and I ran back inside.

I combed the room with my eyes until I found her.
I asked her if she was free in five days
and if I could take her out.

She had eyes that smiled.
She walked like a butterfly flies under an orchid.
She was gorgeous
and had more than four ear piercings
in her right ear.
She was 19 years young with a pierced tongue
and sandy wavy blond hair.

Maybe we would have been friends.
Maybe we would have been lovers.
Maybe nothing.

She lived on the other side of Simpsonville.
Her roommate was a guy
who was sitting on a substantial amount of weight-
pounds of dope, ounces of coke
and stacks of cash
that would make banks be jealous.

He, her, and everyone else in the house
that night
had a bullet pass though their brain
while they were dreaming.

Gloria will not wake up.
She will dream forever.

I think back to that night
when I went to see Swing at the Peace Center
But
instead this time
I daydream that the empty chair to my left

is occupied by Gloria's smiling Easter eyes.
She is wearing a long pea green dress
which hugs her hips.

Her lipstick is a halo rose red.
Her hair drapes
like closing curtains over her tan shoulders.

We stand when the show is over
to give a standing ovation
with the rest of the audience.
We're both applauding.
The grin on my face is sliced ear to ear
and I am happy
because I am here
with her.

Severe Eye Contact With An Old Soul

Lately I've been sleeping
too much.

I've been keeping
in touch
with people
I used to keep at arm's
length.

Everything is constantly
changing
and spinning.

The sky is right.
The ground is left.

Depth perception lessons.
Everything becomes
flat
but close.

So close the soul is exposed.

Depth perception
is gone.

We become transparent
and we become one.
Our faces collide
and our brains
are on top of each other.

Wind cannot blow us apart
because we left our bodies
thirty seconds ago.

Everything I've ever done
is happening now
and I'm getting
what I've been giving.

Dirty House

My house is so funky
there is
carpet

but
my
floors are hardwood.

Lazy Zen Poem 13

This is a dream
I can't sleep or I'll wake up.

Mardi Gras?

Did you know
they measure
the success
of Mardi Gras
in New Orleans
by how many
pounds of trash
they clean
off the streets?

I hear
it gets
knee deep.

H.S.T. Concept in New Orleans

I'm in New Orleans
sipping mango iced tea
in the business district.

There is a moment in a
hostel you might experience
if you ever stay in one.

It's kind of like this
shit,
I need to leave feeling.

This fear of the rubber sack
(Hunter S. Thompson)
came to me
after waiting on the shower
and using no soap
and then eating cold
spicy potatoes for breakfast

Then I decided it was time to go.

Lazy Zen Poem 14

Last night at a jazz club
I heard a trombone sound like a helicopter.

Hot Sex

We could
take our
cloths off,

but that
wouldn't be
enough.

We must
take our
skin off

when we
fuck.

Questions Of Death

I want to write
love notes
on blood soaked
sidewalks
and walk beside
my past life
so I can ask me
how I died
then me would
look up
with
one eye
wide shut
and me would
tell I
that I
fell off a rooftop
from ten stories up
and still
lived to spill
rose colored
love out of
both eardrums
while my adams apple
flapped and
the seam of my skin
pulled open to expose
an overcooked windpipe
and an iron lung deflated

daydreams of
childhood

race by
as I
slam both feet
on the brake
and slide
through an intersection
as if my tires
were skis

my forehead steel mallets
through the windshield

I've been killed
however I choose
to die
my past life snaps back

Solace Through Spoken Word

God forgive us for justice.
God forgive us our trespasses
as we forgive those
who trespass against us.

Combat units
broadcast broadband on Comcast.
The forecast calls for more blasts.

We've just got a Fox News exclusive,
all American soldiers exposed to DU back in 92
will be given purple hearts.

Tomorrow will be partly cloudy
with a 70% chance of retaliation.
Thanks Dan.
Back to you Tom.

Foreign ambassadors are assassinated
for trespassing in their own embassies.
See them bleed live on NBC
tonight at 8.

The sky rains bombs.
Sit back and enjoy the show.

I remember asking people
where you going when the bombs drop?
Well, they did drop.
You want to know where I went?

I went to a poetry reading.

I needed to go to church to find god.
I needed fellowship, and a kind head nod,
A hug and some love from the ones I call family
Poets, MC's, DJ's and B-boys
and all those that are relevant
in a progressive literary movement called slam.

I needed a community.
I needed immunity from the mass media.
Maybe through spoken word I can find solace
and through all this
I have to remember not to
get caught up in the fatalism of human nature.
Just have faith in faith
and keep what's important, important.

As long as I believe in sight
I should be able to see the light.

But I was raised in the age of information
where the Internet paved the way
for instant communication.

Since then, we as a people
have spent more time losing focus
than we have gaining brain waves.
The painstaking process of deciphering
what life means is upon us.

There is no past.
There is no future.
There is only now.
and what you choose to do with it.

This goes out to the cipher on the corner,
to the kid who died talking shit
now he's rhyming to the coroner.

This goes out to the fourteen year old kid
locked in his room.
So pissed off he's bout to rip his ears off
tear drops smear the ink on the page
and the first line reads.
"I get madder than a mad hatter
when I'm around you dad."

Poetry will save that kid.
I know, he was me.

So join hands with a man from a foreign land.

God forgive us for justice,
forgive us our trespasses
as we forgive those
who trespass against us.

Body Language

There is a shadow on the wall
chasing another shadow
in the moonlight.

The motions
make more noise
than the choice
words spoken.

Rise

cold sheets in a dorm room

storm soon
gray skies

the moon dies

waves rise

tides collide with individuality

and stay up.

waves bust
sand and shells
rush through
wristwatches
attached to arms of armed guards.

focus low frequencies
to each and every energy in the vicinity
and the bubble will pop.

pop tops pop off
clocks stop
power off
soda can explode
hands shed skin.

each and every capable person
jumps out of the mouth of a
trampoline.

bring the children to god
cause that is where the portal is.

we all jump in a foam machine
in the middle of the woods.

frogs get as big as artic polar bears
and we are the flies.
insects fly by with nine inch wingspans.
we can't stand seven feet deep in the mud
we hide under rocks
we burrow holes
curl up
in the darkness
and wait in our cocoon.

when we hatch
we exhale thoughts
and get pushed into the sidewalk.

freeze frame.
kodak.
camera flash.
we hold back
we hold back
we hold back
then we inhale
and bring the beige sky closer
closer to where horoscopes
scope us out in our anthill.

My People Are Poets

My people struggle.

My people hustle with muscle
Monday to Sunday.

My people need to eat
speak, spit and sleep.

My people sleep in hostels
and spit lyrics for ears
whether they hear it or not.

Voices carry microphones
back to the homeland.

I've seen a man
hold the spirit of the holy ghost
in one hand
his own soul in the other hand
and when that man clapped he smashed
both balls of light together
and the seas divided
and the trees uprooted
and the roots were Medusa's snakes
and there was a magnificent
shake in the hearts of men.

The audience couldn't applaud.
They were limestone stuck.

My people are poets.

Poets push in penitentiaries.
Poets overthrow the powers that be.

Poets keep keeping
  on on
the streets at
  dawn.

preaching psalms from
bibles that they wrote,
broke, cold and hungry
for sanity.

Poets will endure.
Poets will push and push
until they give birth
to the perfect version of a poem,
revising above an angry moon
looking down at the only world they know.

My people hoist a clenched fist
and sail through the inferno, unscathed.

My people don't die before death.

To spit lightning you must walk
through the thunder.

In A World Of Pimps And Hoes

In a world of pimps and hoes
broke bitches and bosses with limps sit.

Everybody's got problems to fix,
fixes to fix
tricks to turn
and money to make.

Eighteen year olds creep in
with a mission
to slip a ten in
a sparkly G string.

"She seems nice
but *that* bitch is *too* fat
I don't know,
I like a Kate Moss
looking slut with her elbows
poking out of her skin."
He says to his friends.

They don't hide their erections.
They get lap dances.

There are no limits
but everybody's got lines they won't cross.
At least they used to,
some of these bitches and tricks
crossed about every line
on the highway high and drunk
driving home every night.

In a world of pimps and hoes
everything goes.
Dollars are traded for favors.
"Fuck off I'm not willing to do that
unless you blow me or raise the price!"

In a world of pimps and hoes
everybody's got a price
and there's always a man in a wool suit
in the back with more cash than God
and there's always the finest woman
this side of a nighttime nightmare
that won't fuck you for any price.

Is He Gay?

One of my favorite poets
is Jason Carney.

If you ever hear this guy's work
you'll know he's coming from a different angle.

At the regional poetry slam
in New Orleans on finals night
at the House of Blues
Jason kissed me on the cheek
and then whispered in my ear,
"The chick in a red dress is really a dude."

I turned to look at the two women
he was gesturing at and yes,

she did look like a man.

He leaned in again and said softly,
"I'm going to fuck her in her ass
while her friend watches."

He introduced me to a
fine woman in a flower print dress
and the questionable gender in a red dress.
Names were exchanged.

Then I said, "You know
Jason likes caesar salads
but he *really loves* tossed salads."
They giggled.

Then I explained that it was
just a joke and I didn't mean it
and Jason wasn't gay.

Then we all had a good laugh.

I freaked them out
or maybe they saw someone they knew
on the other side of the room
and went over to talk to them
but they left.

Jason told me
I owed him a shot for scaring his pussy away.

I told him
I was going to write a poem
about what just happened.

He said I couldn't publish it unless
I said he had a twelve inch cock
to please the ladies with.

So here you go Jason.
You have a twelve inch cock
to please the ladies with.

Ground Control To Lost Soul

ground control to lost soul
ground control to lost soul
if you copy
come in lost soul
come in lost soul
we have lost contact

protocol told it all
fall in line and fall behind
all the minds gathered around
the TV set
in the living room
just died
TV sets set standards
channel surfers demand further inspections

and yesterday a pentecostal christian lady
asked me
if I want to be saved
she said I was not a spiritual being
and I don't know Jesus
and I said excuse me miss
but you don't know me
she said what if you're wrong baby
I'll pray for you

I asked if her faith was based
on fear tactics after I heard her
pastor condemn faggots
and fundamentalist Muslims
who die for what they believe
wasn't Jesus a religious martyr?

I seek answers but am I asking the right questions?
I go to the beach with hopes that she
Mother Nature will teach me
I am barefoot and my toes sink into the soft sand
and I stare off into the horizon
where the ocean meets the sky
and I raise my arms
and I close my eyes
and I listen within to a silent wind
that blows breezes of insights
between my own temples.

but I think
that mankind must have an Oedipus complex
because we want to kill our grandfather clock's history
and shake the hands of time backwards
we want to sex our mother nature
until there is no life cycle left to be pedaled

suspend time
the mind is endless
spirit is infinite
limits don't exist

be a beacon of light
be the wind that blows the leaves
don't be the leaves being blown by the wind
and beware of pride
it is the deadliest of the seven deadly sins

stand up and be counted
climb a mountain
be a devout believer in now
you are her now
don't take short cuts
life can be cut short

let your instinct guide you as a compass
you are not the things you buy
you are not the drink you sip
you are not the poem you spit
you are not the car you drive
edgar allen poe said
all you see
and all you seem
is a dream
within a dream

so will I look between my eyebrows
palms up
back straight
legs crossed
breathe deep
and I will float
I will float

we will wrap ourselves in the blankets of the clouds
we will lounge in the smile of the crescent moon
and hula hoop Saturn's rings
we will dance on the surface of the sun
look at the earth beneath us
and breath star dust
we will jump from planet to planet
and ride a shooting star
into the other side
of the never ending sunset

the messiah is crying in the maternity ward
the messiah is crying in the maternity ward

if man is made in God's image
then every infant is baby Jesus

I seek answers but am I asking the right questions?
I go to the beach with hopes that she
Mother Nature will teach me
I am barefoot and my toes sink into the soft sand
and I stare off into the horizon
where the ocean meets the sky
and I raise my arms
and I close my eyes
and I listen within to a silent wind
that blows breezes of insights
between my own temples.

but I think
that mankind must have an Oedipus complex
because we want to kill our grandfather clock's history
and shake the hands of time backwards
we want to sex our mother nature
until there is no life cycle left to be pedaled

suspend time
the mind is endless
spirit is infinite
limits don't exist

be a beacon of light
be the wind that blows the leaves
don't be the leaves being blown by the wind
and beware of pride
it is the deadliest of the seven deadly sins

stand up and be counted
climb a mountain
be a devout believer in now
you are her now
don't take short cuts
life can be cut short

let your instinct guide you as a compass
you are not the things you buy
you are not the drink you sip
you are not the poem you spit
you are not the car you drive
edgar allen poe said
all you see
and all you seem
is a dream
within a dream

so will I look between my eyebrows
palms up
back straight
legs crossed
breathe deep
and I will float
I will float

we will wrap ourselves in the blankets of the clouds
we will lounge in the smile of the crescent moon
and hula hoop Saturn's rings
we will dance on the surface of the sun
look at the earth beneath us
and breath star dust
we will jump from planet to planet
and ride a shooting star
into the other side
of the never ending sunset

the messiah is crying in the maternity ward
the messiah is crying in the maternity ward

if man is made in God's image
then every infant is baby Jesus

we journey through theories delirious
searching through mirrors
to find endearing eyes on the other side
and we cry burgundy tears out of fear
but what we seek is here
inside of us

plus and divide by love
it is the only factor that matters
so I will wipe my eyes
and thank god
for telling me to ask why

ground control to lost soul
ground control to lost soul
if you copy
come in lost soul
come in lost soul
we just lost contact

ABOUT GREATUNPUBLISHED.COM

www.greatunpublished.com is a website that exists to serve writers and readers, and to remove some of the commercial barriers between them. When you purchase a GreatUNpublished title, whether you order it in electronic form or in a paperback volume, the author is receiving a majority of the post-production revenue.

A GreatUNpublished book is never out of stock, and always available, because each book is printed on-demand, as it is ordered.

A portion of the site's share of profits is channeled into literacy programs.

So by purchasing this title from GreatUNpublished, you are helping to revolutionize the publishing industry for the benefit of writers and readers.

And for this we thank you.